EXTREME BEAUTY: THE BODY TRANSFORMED

EXTREME BEAUTY: THE BODY TRANSFORMED

Harold Koda

The Metropolitan Museum of Art, New York

Yale University Press, New Haven and London

This volume has been published in conjunction with the exhibition "Extreme Beauty: The Body Transformed," held at The Metropolitan Museum of Art from December 6, 2001, through March 3, 2002.

Published by The Metropolitan Museum of Art, New York

John P. O'Neill, Editor in Chief
Gwen Roginsky, Associate General Manager of Publications
Barbara Cavaliere, Editor
Design by Takaaki Matsumoto, Matsumoto Incorporated, New York
Elisa Frohlich, Production Manager

Library of Congress Cataloging-in-Publication Data
Koda, Harold
Extreme beauty: the body transformed / Harold Koda.
        p.   cm.
    Catalogue accompanying an exhibition at The Metropolitan Museum of Art, New York from Dec. 6, 2001 through March 3, 2002.
        ISBN 1-58839-014-4 (hc. : alk. Paper)—
        ISBN 1-58839-015-2 (pbk. : alk. paper)
        ISBN 0-300-09117-6 (Yale univ.)
        1. Costume—History—Exhibitions.
    2. Beauty, Personal—Cross-cultural studies—Exhibitions. I. Metropolitan Museum of Art (New York, N.Y.) II. Costume Institute (New York, N.Y.) III. Title.

GT503 .K63 2001
391'.074'7471—dc21   2001044709

Color separations by Professional Graphics Inc., Rockford, Illinois
Printed by Brizzolis Arte en Gráficas, Madrid
Bound by Encuadernación Ramos, S.A., Madrid
Printing and binding coordinated by Ediciones El Viso, S.A., Madrid

Cover: Junya Watanabe, Dress with neck ruff, "Techno Couture" collection, fall-winter 2000. Photograph: Firstview.com

Frontispiece: South Africa, Three unmarried Ndebele girls, 1976-82. Photograph: Natalie Knight Productions cc.

CONTENTS

FOREWORD

The exhibition "Extreme Beauty: The Body Transformed" and the accompanying volume mark Harold Koda's welcome return to The Metropolitan Museum of Art, as Curator in Charge of The Costume Institute. He was previously Associate Curator and the colleague for many years of the Institute's late Curator, Richard Martin. Together, these esteemed partners established a unique and enlightening tradition, using fashion as the basis to present new insights into historical and cultural issues and brilliantly showing how these insights resonate in contemporary fashion. Koda continues that wonderful tradition and brings to it his own unique ideas.

Extreme Beauty addresses the ideals of beauty that have persisted or shifted through the ages in various cultures. The mechanisms of costume have transformed the zones of the body, dictating shaping and proportion by artificially changing the body's silhouette and sometimes physically altering its natural structure. Koda draws on the historical and cultural diversity of fashion to tell the fascinating complex story of the continual varied shifts of style and recurrences of the past that have occurred right up to the present. His project is especially pertinent in this age, when mass communication enables individuals around the globe to reach through time and across cultures by jet or by computer. He examines historical fashions, traditional costuming from Africa and Asia, and fashions by some of the most creative and often controversial designers of today—John Galliano for Christian Dior, Alexander McQueen for Givenchy, Rei Kawakubo for Comme des Garçons, Issey Miyake, and Thierry Mugler, among others.

Koda also mined the resources of other departments in the Metropolitan Museum to find wonderful and often surprising art-historical evidence in support of his subject in paintings, sculptures, prints, photographs, and armor. A number of caricatures provide humorous and pertinent interpretations of the lengths—and heights—to which fashion has gone to create ideals of style. In addition to the changes rendered by fashion's intervention, *Extreme Beauty* incorporates works that show how the nude body has been subjected to physical manipulation in the desire to make it more beautiful.

Each of the book's five chapters covers a major part of the body—the neck and shoulders, chest, waist, hips, and feet. The introductions provide a chronological look at the history of each zone, and the pages that follow feature intriguing juxtapositions of texts and images. Unique comparisons are made, showing both connections and differences. In the chapter on the neck and shoulders, for example, the early seventeenth-century ruff is portrayed in an engraving of the period and in an oil by Cornelis de Vos, both in the Metropolitan's collection. These are shown with an ensemble of 2001 by the Japanese designer Yoshiki Hishinuma. The three images exhibit a strikingly similar effect: the head seems to float above the body at a greater than natural distance. The extended necks of a Burmese Padaung woman and of a South African Ndebele woman share a picture spread with an X ray that shows the physical effects of Burmese neck coils on the bones of their wearers.

This ingeniously inventive synthesis of apparel's role in the continuing manipulation of the body ideal raises thought-provoking issues, which we hope will encourage future scholarship. *Extreme Beauty: The Body Transformed* also addresses the old saying "Beauty is in the eye of the beholder." It offers contemporary beholders an opportunity to look beyond their own preconceived notions about ideal beauty and to consider that what is often perceived as extreme can also be beautiful.

Philippe de Montebello
Director
The Metropolitan Museum of Art

INTRODUCTION

Fashion's great seduction is its mutability. Through the artifice of apparel, the less than perfect can camouflage perceived deficiencies and in some instances project an appeal beyond those gifted with characteristics accepted as ideal in their culture and time. However, while fashion is commonly thought to be driven by a constant cycle of aspiration and obsolescence, the ideal unclothed body paradoxically is believed to conform to some unchanging and universal standard. In fact, an examination of the nude in art reveals a constant if sometimes subtle shift in the ideal of physical beauty.

In art historian Kenneth Clark's definition, the nude is the naked body clothed in culture. In sculpture and painting, it can be seen to manifest certain meanings and ideals as explicitly as the body clothed. Costume historian Anne Hollander argues persuasively that the nude is even more directly expressive of its time than Clark proposes. Hollander sets forth the premise that the naked body is rendered in art as if it retains the imprint of its dress: although clothing has been shed, the nude body has been cast in its mold.

Both Clark and Hollander perceive the body as evidence of pan-cultural phenomena. Hollander's argument especially presupposes that culturally bound aesthetic biases override the more specific conditions of artistic ability and intentions, or the artist's idiosyncratic predilections. On cursory viewing, the *Venus of Willendorf*, shown on the facing page, might appear to be a highly stylized rendering of an exaggeratedly obese female form. But closer study suggests that the depiction is not necessarily so stylized or abstract as to preclude a literal representational intention. The Willendorf Venus may deviate from the classical norm, but she is not so exaggerated as to preclude a human model. While the radical foreshortening of her lower legs and her thin atrophied arms are details that do not appear to conform to the rest of her remarkable *avoirdupois*, the Willendorf Venus is arguably a faithful description of an endomorphic type. At very least, she represents a cluster of characteristics that warranted, to an artist of her time, a patient rendering in stone.

Art often depicted the nude with the invisible impress of apparel, but the advent of photography muted the effect of a contemporary ideal of the dressed form on the naked body. The disjunction between a representation of the clothed and fashionable beauty and the naked artist's model, or *demi-mondaine*, was emphasized further by the use of retouching on the clothed figure to make the desirable attributes of beauty more clearly apparent. This practice is seen in images of the famed Countess Castiglione from the 1860s, in photogravures from fashion publications at the beginning of the twentieth century, and it continues to this day. But if art and photography no longer document the more recent variations of a period ideal in their representations of the nude, other artifacts support the proposition that cultural perceptions of physical attractiveness are mutable. In the twentieth century, when most renowned artists repudiated figurative expression, the physical ideal and its accelerating variability can be witnessed in dress forms and display mannequins, fashion's surrogates for the contemporary body.

In the first decade of the 1900s, mannequins were rendered with fleshy shoulders and arms, not too different in effect from an Ingres odalisque. Unlike Ingres' painted nudes, however, mannequins were severely pinched in at the waist, and the bust, while ample, betrayed no cleavage and hung low on the ribcage. The hipline flared at the sides in an hourglass shape that was shifted off its vertical axis, with the chest pushed forward and the hips pulled back. While the fin-de-siècle standards of beauty persisted into the first two decades of the twentieth century, they were attended by an emerging cult of slenderness. The new narrowed line of the female form was still softly modeled, but an overall slimness abided.

By the 1920s, the body's curves were renounced and a cult of thinness was in such dramatic ascendance that it alarmed even Paul Poiret, who had ostensibly introduced it. Commenting on the paradigm shift, the designer declared, "Formerly women were architectural, like the prows of ships, and very beautiful. Now they resemble little under-nourished telegraph clerks." But even in the 1920s, when the planarity of the flapper look predominated, display mannequins and fashion models, though somewhat more attenuated in proportion than in the past, continued to project a rounded softness. No collarbones or sinewy musculature were admitted to the canon of feminine beauty, despite the period's preference for a linear silhouette. It was not until the 1930s that mannequins begin to convey a less fleshy aspect, and it is at this point that an overall thinness distinguished from any other historical period prevailed. The shoulders were squared and the clavicle was decisively articulated for the first time. While the mannequins of the 1920s suggested a body unconstrained by foundation garments, the new ectomorphic mannequins of the 1930s, particularly by the end of the decade, were sculpted with a defined waist and hipline alluding to a renewed practice of corsetry and girdling.

Mannequins of the World War II years and the period immediately following have high conical breasts, a small waist, and a suppressed hipline. In this period, it was the hipline that was most altered from its predecessor. With the introduction of historicist styles by Christian Dior in 1947, the ideal form was endowed with a greater pulchritude at the bust and hips, and the waist was indented more emphatically. The relative naturalism of the body that characterized the period from the 1920s until the war was renounced. The stomach and buttocks were flattened, but the outline of the hips was emphasized and enhanced by padding or small panniers. Unlike the corseted posture of the past, which was vertical or S curved, the New Look stance was characterized by a long rounded back with the buttocks tucked under and the pelvis jutted forward. In the mid-1950s, Cristobal Balenciaga re-introduced the chemise silhouette with his "Sack" dress, providing an alternative to the body-defining style of the post-war period. It was not until the 1960s, however, that a new ideal of the body was established.

The transcendent body type of the 1960s was characterized by an adolescent androgyny and angularity. Arms and legs were thinner and elongated. Significantly, the gestures and postures of fashion models of the period, and consequently of display mannequins as well, were more expressive and less static than they had been in the past. The cocked hip, legs, and arms-akimbo stances favored in the period underscored the relatively unencumbered nature of the body. By the end of the 1960s, the mannequin sculptor's acknowledgment of the sea change occurring in the aesthetics of the fashionable body could be observed in the depiction of the bust as if unsupported by a brassiere.

Mannequins in the 1970s were invariably represented with breasts somewhat pendant and asymmetrical in profile. In addition, an innovation within the fashion world from the 1960s, the incorporation of a heterogeneous culturally inclusive concept of beauty was securely established. African, Asian, and Southern European models had broken through the exclusionary barriers of a homogeneous Northern European standard. With individual characteristics taken from life, often of fashion models, display mannequins began to support the notion of an eclectic range of physical types that might be considered beautiful. Despite this apparent expanding of criteria for the beautiful form, certain prejudices continued. The ideal was still obdurately one of youth and thinness. With the cultural relaxation of rules of appropriate body exposure, a universal standard of beauty became increasingly problematic, no matter how inclusive it was in relation to the past. The refuge of wearing foundation garments to re-form the body was obsolete, and

Gravettian culture, *Venus of Willendorf*, stone, Upper Palaeolithic Period, ca. 30,000-18,000 B.C. Naturhistorisches Museum, Vienna. Photograph: Copyright Erich Lessing / Art Resource, New York

Greek, *Aphrodite of Knidos,* antique replica of original by Praxiteles, marble, ca. 350 B.C. Musée du Louvre, Paris. Photograph: Copyright Erich Lessing / Art Resource, New York

the greater tyranny emerged of an ideal of beauty with the impossibility of recourse to artifice. In no other century has the ideal form of the body been in such flux. And at no other time since the fourteenth century have the fashionably dressed had to transform their bodies to the rigorous standards of the nude without apparel's assist.

The past twenty years have witnessed an extraordinarily diverse production of designs that have coincided with general trends in the arts, with post-modern, feminist, structuralist and deconstuctivist approaches predominating. At the same time that the fashion world has accommodated increasingly conceptual designs, the arts have seen a compatible assimilation of some of the most fundamental issues addressed by fashion: the body, gender, personal narratives, and the mechanism of commerce and production. And many recent contemporary art exhibitions have addressed the questions of what constitutes beauty and whether beauty itself should continue to be of relevance or concern to the artist.

More than fifty years ago, the Museum of Modern Art presented a show on fashion curated by architect and social critic Bernard Rudofsky. The theme was "Are Clothes Modern." From the perspective and premises of modernism, many of the garments and ornaments of the body over time and across cultures were seen as illogical and unreasonable. The clear bias of the exhibition was for clothing that did not constrain the body, while fulfilling its functional and social requirements. Ornament was not exactly abjured, but clearly, all the modernist impulses aligned with an aesthetic of material and structural integrity resulted in a relatively restrained vocabulary. "Are Clothes Modern" tacitly endorsed non-tailored folk and regional dress, and sportswear by such designers as Claire McCardell and Bonnie Cashin. These Americans were known for prioritizing function: their clothing was conceived as assembled separates and was intended to free the wearer's movements. The thinking behind their apparel expressed many of the beliefs of early twentieth-century modernist artists and architects.

Rudofsky sought to purge fashion of its irrational aspects. Although his critique had the faint moralizing tone of a proscription, his prime argument was the perceived unhealthiness of many of fashion's conventions. By situating his rationalist argument in this way, Rudofsky aligned himself with many of the dress reformers of the nineteenth century. The idea that apparel might be so extreme as to compromise the health of the fashionable wearer has recently been subject to reassessment. Valerie Steele, working with Dr. Lynn Kutsche, has come to the startling conclusion that much of the literature describing the deleterious nature of corsetry is unsupportable by medical evidence. With forensic acuity, they have refuted or corrected the suspect descriptions of the surgical removal of lower ribs, the penetration of the lungs and other organs by broken ribs, anemia, miscarriages, and bifurcated livers. Similarly, the Golden Lotus, or Chinese foot-binding, has come under recent scrutiny and reevaluation by historians. Although the physical trauma effected by the long tradition of foot-binding is irrefutable, new scholarship has expunged much of the lurid apocrypha from its history. More surprisingly, some post-feminist readings have ascribed a positive psycho-social role to the practice of foot-binding in Chinese culture.

Basic to Rudofsky's approach is the notion that the body has an ideal natural form. With the modernist's conviction, he presumed that beauty resided in all things natural and therefore that naturalness was to be preserved even in dress. But, for Rudofsky, the natural body conformed to an ideal that originated in classical antiquity. His foil for the innumerable eccentricities embraced by humanity was invariably from the ancient canon, portrayed by sculptors such as Polykleitos, Lysippus, and Praxiteles. In fact, the classical female nude is "natural" in that it does not reflect the constrictions of the body that, with the advent of tailored dress, have been adumbrated so commonly in nudes in Western art. But, even in the *Aphrodite of Knidos,* reproduced on the left, and the *Apollo Belvedere,* shown on the facing page, cultural prejudices abide, as can be seen in the physical variations of the classical type.

Salomon Reinach, an early twentieth-century archaeologist associated with the Ecole du Louvre, attempted to establish a standard for dating statuary based on the proportions of the breasts and their relative positioning, which he called *indices mammaire.* Reinach believed that smaller widely spaced breasts could be seen to increase in diameter as well as to shift closer together over time. In his view, their dilation and proximity evolved with enough predictability that a chronology could be extrapolated. While disputed by scholars, his system of codification of classical proportions was not isolated. The imposition of a geometrically proportional system to establish the characteristics of beauty originates from the ancient Greeks and has a long tradition in Western art. The most famous example is Leonardo's *Vitruvian Man,* which conforms to Vitruvius' incomplete description of the lost Polykleitan canon. The Renaissance reliance on the proportions of ancient classical models has been a persistent standard of the ideal human form.

The notion of one canon applied to the diversity of human types, even within broadly defined racial groups, is one of the mechanisms for prejudice that fashion has been able to diffuse. In 1999, the American Museum of Natural History held the exhibition "Body Art: Marks of Identity." In contrast to "Are Clothes Modern," this show documented a variety of techniques of body manipulation and used anthropological and ethnographic methodologies to contexualize rather than critique the various practices. The same year, the Kyoto Costume Institute's "Visions of the Body: Body Images and Fashion in the 20th Century" addressed contemporary expressions of the human form through dress by focusing on the high fashion system. Organized by Akiko Fukai, this exhibition presented a comprehensive survey of the international avant-garde. Ethnographic material was not included, but a prologue of period foundation garments and costumes situated the contemporary material historically.

Earlier this year, the designer Walter van Beirendonck was responsible for an exhibition titled "Mutilate," which cited examples of transformative dress from various cultures and time periods. While "Mutilate" focused on many of the issues and objects treated in *Extreme Beauty*, it addressed as well the techniques of body manipulation central to the Museum of Natural History's "Body Art" show.

Roman copy after Greek original, *Apollo Belvedere,* marble, ca. 350–320 B.C. Museo Pio Clementino, Vatican Museums, Vatican State. Photograph: Copyright Scala / Art Resource, New York

Extreme Beauty originated in part from a discussion about the competitive nature of fashion. In many historical instances, details of dress appear to evolve with increasing exaggeration until they are unsupportable and implode. It can be argued that the only mechanism for the demise of a faddish style is the physical limit of the body to suffer its intervention. The notion of a fashionable ideal that becomes more mannered over time due to one-upmanship is appealing in its simplicity: fashion as extreme sport. However, a review of historical fashion trends cannot sustain this argument as the sole motivation for fashion's elaboration on its own sometimes perplexing forms. Many instances exist in which an inconvenient or simply purely ornamental form persists relatively unchanged for generations. In the case of Chinese foot-binding, the practice is thought to have endured for almost a millennium.

Extreme Beauty is organized around five zones of the body: the neck and shoulders, the chest, the waist, the hips, and the feet. It concentrates on the way differing times and cultures achieve variations from the ostensibly normative condition of the naked body, with clothing as the mechanism for the reformation of the body rather than cosmetics, body scarification, hair treatments, and other mechanisms of alteration that are not clearly apparel. There is no doubt that much of the material has a multitude of meanings and intentions: displays of status, wealth, power, gender, cultivation, ceremony, and group affiliations. While acknowledging the validity of current cultural, ethnographic, sociographic, and theoretical approaches, *Extreme Beauty* proposes that a direct formal analyses of the strategies employed to create an aesthetic ideal may also yield new insights on the concept of fashionable beauty.

Like the Surrealists' game of the *cadavre exquis*, or the exquisite corpse, *Extreme Beauty* addresses each zone of the body in discrete isolation. This division of the body into parts results in the *cadavre exquis'* peculiar and often monstrous combinations. But the dissection and reorganization should not obscure the fact that fashions are invariably about the whole figure and the coordination of proportions for final effect. Most commonly, as in Elizabethan England, fashion is the amalgamation of all the zones—face-framing collar, suppressed bust, dilated shoulders, corseted and attenuated waist, farthingaled hips, and narrow shoes with heels. In another instance, the fifteenth-century fop who affected pointed-toed *poulaines* was also dressed in a doublet with shoulders widened by padded sleeves and a narrowly cinched waist made smaller in effect by a short but full heavily pleated skirt. Although one zone may be the focus of a period or culture, any extreme intervention is often accompanied or balanced by other manipulations of the body's proportions.

Certain extraordinary fashion collections of the past twenty-five years have introduced an increasingly conceptually driven approach that has animated the field. The designs that are the core of *Extreme Beauty* appear to be manifestations of change in the relationship of fashion to society. Certainly, contemporary expressions of dress have exceeded historical precedents: John Galliano's gown is wider than the broadest panniered dress from the eighteenth century, and its train is longer than the crinoline hooped skirts of the 1860s; Mr. Pearl's corseted waist is smaller than any of the corsets represented here, save one of an interesting and disputed authenticity; and Walter van Beirendonck's stilts or Alexander McQueen's prosthetics far exceed the heights of sixteenth-century Venetian *chopines*. While many of the most elaborate idea-driven designs are never seen on the street, they are invariably crucial to the promotion of a more diluted "realistic" product. This design process, freed from the requirement for only the quotidian, functional, and accessible, has generated more purely aesthetic and conceptual, as opposed to market-driven,

Peter Paul Rubens, *The Three Graces*, detail, oil on canvas, 17th century. Museo del Prado, Madrid. Photograph: Copyright Scala / Art Resource, NY

forms. As contemporary artists have engaged increasingly in issues related to the body and dress, fashion has demonstrated an analogous assimilation of critical theories.

Many of the more provocative designs have come from Japan, Great Britain, and Belgium. In the 1970s, Issey Miyake introduced a conceptual approach to fashion informed by contemporary art issues rather than by clothing trends. He established that the making of clothing could have the intellectual and aesthetic resonance of the other arts. Often described as a kind of origami, Miyake's designs, though highly engineered, projected a process of intuitive draping rather than tailoring. Miyake, who has often used the body as an armature without a conventional disclosure of the body's form, is the first of the international designers to propose a silhouette at variance with all that had preceded it. In the early 1980s, other Japanese designers extended Miyake's novel notion of dress and the body. The fashion avant-garde was galvanized by their aesthetic, devoid of color or sheen and without body-conscious or body-revealing cuts. Rei Kawakubo for Comme des Garçons and Yohji Yamamoto transformed the fashion discourse with their layered all-black collections. As their careers have evolved, neither has compromised the initial shocking originality of their design proposals. Perhaps the aptness of their work for *Extreme Beauty* is, as Brigid Foley of *W* said of Kawakubo, that the designer "shows us beauty where we did not know it existed." Like the work of many artists at the end of the twentieth century, the Japanese designers subvert the relationship of the beautiful to the ugly. More than others, they have established that fashion can invest the plain, the mundane, and sometimes the unattractive with aesthetic power. Other Japanese designers, including Junko Koshino, Junya Watanabe, and Yoshiki Hishinuma, have introduced the hyper-kinetic imagery of Shinjuku and Shibuya neon, anime (Japanese shorthand for animation), and the often lurid effects of Japanese toys and street crafts into their beautifully rendered designs. While the earlier Japanese worked for a time in natural fibers and materials with an inherent rustic quality, they have also come to embrace the unabashedly man-made materials that are central to the designs of their younger cohorts.

Beginning with Vivienne Westwood, a number of British designers have enlivened the fashion world with their paradoxical combination of historical affinities and seditionist impulse. Like Westwood, John Galliano and Alexander McQueen refer to historical periods but combine them in ironic Postmodern constructions. What distinguishes the work of these designers is their insistence on the recognizability of each reference in juxtaposition rather than the blurring of sources through synthesis. Also, the politically inflected work of Westwood, McQueen, and Hussein Chalayan addresses the body as a contested site of innumerable narratives: Westwood's repudiation of persistent Victorian prudery; McQueen's images of survivors of psychic, sexual, or political abuse; and Chalayan's critique of the body as a carrier of conservative cultural meanings through adulterated forms of Islamic dress.

Several members of the Antwerp Six, a group of designers who graduated from the Antwerp Academy, as well as other individualistic Belgian designers who followed, have extended the parameters of design by revising the conventions of dress and revisiting definitions of beauty. Their work is characterized by the use of mundane but often unexpected materials—felt, rubber, plastic—and by the exercise of extraordinary technical facility applied in ways that allude to but revise the traditional conventions of tailoring and draping. The work of such designers as Walter van Beirendonck and Martin Margiela and the design teams A. F. Vandervorst and Victor and Rolf have contributed a Dada-like sensibility to contemporary design.

Since the eighteenth century, the French have launched the most surprising manipulations of the body, often rationalized as an ameliorating artifice. In the mid-twentieth century, Christian Dior, Jacques Fath, and Cristobal Balenciaga repudiated the natural lines of the body by citing eighteenth- and nineteenth-century silhouettes. Coco Chanel dismissed the elaborate constructions proposed for women by her fellow male designers with the quip, "A garment must be logical. . . . Men were not meant to dress women." Despite her criticism of the encumbering historicist citations of the post-war period, Chanel herself was very directly responsible for promoting the standard of thinness that was far more difficult to achieve by women with the voluptuous Rubensian form immortalized in the painting shown above left. The structuring assist of foundation garments allowed women to approach the period's ideal to an extent that the sweater-like Chanel suit could not. In the tradition of Chanel, Yves Saint Laurent has generally avoided designs that encumber the body. With rare exceptions, his most fantastical references are applied to apparel forms of comfort and ease. On the other hand, Christian Lacroix has embraced some of the archaic forms of body support in bustled bustiers and cuirasse-style evening gowns, often in collaboration with the corsetiere, Mr. Pearl. The architectonic work of Pierre Cardin may be seen to anticipate the built-up forms, and sci-fi preoccupations of Thierry Mugler. Mugler, like Jean Paul Gaultier, is also inspired by the undeniably camp imagery of 1950s and 1960s television and comic books. While Mugler's themes often focus on a utopian classicism and mid-twentieth-century style *übermensch* and *übermädchen*, Gaultier's world is a polyglot bazaar of anachronistic forms and multicultural people. Both play with stereotypes and iconic forms of dress with knowledge and irony. Other designers, such as Tom Ford, Helmut Lang, Olivier Theyskens, and Jeremy Scott, have introduced a tougher contemporary voice to the Paris fashion scene. Their work expresses a full-frontal engagement with issues of gender, explicit and ambiguous sexuality, and trends from sources in high and popular culture.

While many of the historical and ethnographic examples in *Extreme Beauty* reflect a form of dress normative for the time and culture, much of the more recent work is only rarely seen on the street. Although most are intended as wearable apparel, a few are meant simply to project, with an exaggerated clarity, an aesthetic concept of the designer. This has resulted in a proliferation of designs that are increasingly at a remove from the market yet remain at the very basis of the imagery and franchise of the designer and design house. In this context, fashion is able to address more complex and sometimes difficult concepts that are often at odds with the market. This limited estrangement from direct commerce in part contributes to the increasingly expressive nature of much contemporary fashion. The classical canon has been superseded by exercise regimes, as personified by Arnold Schwarzenegger, who is shown on the right at the pinnacle of his body-building career. At present, when pharmacological programs and cosmetic surgery are acceptable alternatives, and the possibility of genetic manipulation is rapidly approaching, the historical vanities and dramatic physical transformations embraced by other people in other times and cultures may no longer be seen as deformations and barbarisms. Fashion is evidence of the human impulse to bring the body closer to an elusive transient ideal, and *Extreme Beauty* manifests both its most extreme aspirations and opportunities.

Arnold Schwarzenegger, 1978.
Photograph: Max Aguilera-Hellweg / Timpix

NECK AND SHOULDERS

Africa, Kenya, Africa, *Turkana Woman*, postcard, ca. 1970s. The Metropolitan Museum of Art, Arts of Africa, Oceania, and the Americas, The Photograph Study Collection, printed and published by John Hinde Limited, Cabinteely, Co. Dublin, Republic of Ireland. Photograph: Robert Goldman

16

Parmigianino, *Madonna with the Long Neck*, oil on wood, ca. 1535. Uffizi, Florence. Photograph: Copyright Scala/Art Resource, New York

Overleaf: Christian Dior Haute Couture, fall-winter 1997. *Princess Afsharid* suit, designed by John Galliano. Photograph: Courtesy of CORBIS

The preference for a long neck is perhaps the only corporeal aesthetic that is universally shared. Canons of beauty have never favored the head bent and lowered into the shoulders by either age or postural adjustment. In all cultures, the head held high is associated with dignity, authority, and well-being. The bias for an aesthetic of youthful nubility is not surprising, but the extension of the prejudice to issues of carriage is not a necessary corollary. Although a tottering walk, widening hips, and thickened waists, for example, may be seen as manifestations of aging or even decrepitude, each has appeared as a standard of fashionable beauty at various times. The preference for a graceful swan-like neck is not restricted to a prioritization of youthfulness over senescence; it also introduces the acculturated aspects of physical bearing and poise.

Obviously, the neck is a place to drape prestigious symbols of wealth and authority. But such displays can also function as a beautifying device to create, for men and women of any age, the illusion of a well-positioned head supported by a graceful or powerful long neck. As seen at the upper left, even as necklaces, collars, and ruffs frame the face, they also serve to ameliorate the effect of the less-than-ideal neck. The most exaggerated accessories of dress related to the neck have invariably incorporated an optical adjustment of the head's relationship to the body's trunk. When ambiguity about the distance from chin to shoulder is introduced, the illusory measure historically has never been a contraction; it has always been a strategy to visually attenuate the neck's length.

Most typically, neckline constructions were accomplished by a minimum of shaping through cut during the early development of tailored garments in the late Middle Ages. Whether rounded, V-shaped, or straight across, necklines were invariably high, opening at most to mid-sternum and never exposing the outer shoulders. The thin gathered edges of chemises and undergarments often peeked from under the outer garments and later evolved into flat collars and ruff-like forms. By the early fifteenth century, the drawstring styles previously pulled up closely to the neck started to loosen. Both Italian and Northern paintings began to depict fashions with more open necklines. In the 1500s, especially in Italian designs, garments reveal the whole of the neck's flare into the trapezius, and in some examples, part of the arm's deltoid cap. This shoulder exposure precipitated another means of lengthening the neck.

Artists of the sixteenth century could use simple license to portray the natural shoulderline supporting an exaggerated neck. In many instances, as exemplified at the lower left, they had the model tip her head to the side or crane in one direction. By so depicting a subject, the artist gave a naturalistic rationale to the longer line of the neck. But in life, the neck, with its fixed number of vertebrae, has its limitations. Since the vertebrae cannot be physically extended, a straightened spine and angled shoulders were affected. Of the two, the dropping of the shoulders to create a line almost coincident with the downward angle of the trapezius was the more transformative. A narrower shoulder is sometimes the consequence of a deviation of the clavicles, which also accentuates the length of the neck. The Ndebele women of South Africa and the Padaung women of Burma wear wire coils that appear to stretch their necks by weighing down their collarbones to artificially induce this physical idiosyncrasy. These body transformations conform, in a more explicit manner, to an aesthetic and a process shared by European women of style from the sixteenth century through much of the nineteenth century. In the later period, the corset with shoulder straps provided the orthopedic assistance required to create a permanently triangulated shoulder.

The transformation of the ideal shoulder slope from perpendicular to a forty-five-degree angle can be seen in seventeenth-century portraits in which van Dyke collars create a straight line from the jaw to the outer shoulder, obscuring any sense of anatomical reality. Even in the absence of a collar as evidenced by nudes of the period, where the neck was reinstated, the trapezius was so emphasized that it absorbed the deltoid in its mass.

This triangulated shoulder became less apparent in the eighteenth century. The corset of the period pulled the arms back, narrowing the back and shoulders. This imposed posture was ensured by the use of a busk, a wooden or metal rod placed down the center front of the corset. The apparent slope of the shoulders was effectively diminished by shrinking their width. But in almost every painting where the neckline is visible, the angle of the trapezius from the base of the neck to the beginning of the deltoid is maintained, smooth and unbroken save for a slight dimpling to indicate the arm socket.

Eighteenth- and nineteenth-century bodices reveal the actual transformation of the upper body through their pattern pieces. In eighteenth-century examples, the shoulder seam was pushed to the back, with the armhole clearly shifted backward. In the nineteenth century, the shoulder seam remained more-or-less in place, but it was canted more obliquely, and the armhole was shifted forward. As a result, the shoulders were so decisively angled that the back-seaming of a tailored nineteenth-century garment took on a diamond-shaped configuration.

The 1830s brought an increasingly broadened back that replicated the severely triangulated form of the Stuart shoulder. This lowered armhole and sloped profile were to persist until the late 1880s, when a narrowed shoulder again returned. In the 1880s, the shoulder seams, although still positioned at the back, began to move upward and were only slightly angled. As was the case earlier, the physical alteration of the body was reflected in the seaming as well. But as the sloped shoulderline—an optical assist to the appearance of an attenuated neck—disappeared, other strategies took its place. The high collar that emerged out of the fashion of the lower band collar reasserted the cylindrical form of the neck as a separate pattern piece. As seen in the portrait at the upper right, a lowered bosom stance later introduced a proportion that visually enhanced the length of the gorge.

The strong broad shoulder is a recurring heroic ideal that can be seen in examples as early as prehistoric wall paintings. However, it was in the twentieth century that a vogue for wide squared shoulders took hold in men's tailoring and womenswear. This mode differs from any other period of the exaggerated shoulder, perhaps because it reflected an earlier trend in menswear. Prior expressions of the wide shoulder had relied on the sleeves burgeoning or the collar expanding rather than on the actual padding out of the shoulder itself, but this changed with Elsa Schiaparelli's introduction of a slightly padded shoulder in 1937. The fashionable ideal of the late 1930s and early 1940s was a dramatic V-shaped torso for both sexes. To accomplish this, large pads wrapped the deltoids, often extending beyond them to support the sleeves in their cantilever. The shoulders' broadness was underscored by a narrowed and flattened hipline, a silhouette abetted by unvented men's jackets and elastic women's girdles.

Although padding in menswear persisted into the 1950s, Christian Dior's historicist 1947 "New Look" collection reintroduced the rounded slope of shoulder, wasp waist, and hip padding last seen in the Belle Epoque. The 1950s woman of style, did not have the advantage of the nineteenth-century corset's shoulder straps to help her achieve the desired angled shoulder. She had to rely on the discipline of posture.

Except for a brief attempt at reintroducing the 1940s silhouette by Yves Saint Laurent in 1971, the extended and squared shoulder did not emerge again until 1979. In womenswear the stronger shoulder suggested the increasing professional authority of the wearer, but it was also a perfect tailoring device. Because the wider shoulder introduced more fabric, it simplified the fitting and shaping to the body, especially over the bust. The shoulder established a smoother fall of the garment and accommodated the balancing of grainlines of the fabric essential to the proper fit and finish of a tailored garment. In its reprise, the big-shouldered silhouette was often balanced by a narrowed waist but a rounded hipline. Contemporary designers like Thierry Mugler and Claude Montana modified the androgynous girdled form of the World War II era and paired their broadened shoulders with the waist and hips redolent of a voluptuous "New Look" femininity. The result was a conflation of mid-century fashion imagery cobbled into designs of Postmodern and post-feminist implication.

There are only a few major instances in fashion that directly address the nape of neck. Various designers have attempted to camouflage the massing of flesh that occurs there. Called the "Dowager's Hump," this condition is associated with the increasing curvature of the spine and the compaction of the vertebrae that attends forms of osteoporosis and normal advanced aging. The great mid-twentieth century Spanish couturier Cristobal Balenciaga came up with a solution. Rather than raise the neckline at back, which only made the head appear to bend further into the shoulders, Balenciaga curved the collar away from the body and exposed the neck. For him, the ostensible disfigurement was thus transformed into a long gracefully padded curve.

The Japanese have focused on the nape of the neck as an important point of a woman's beauty. As shown at the lower right, the back neckline of the kimono is carved away to attenuate the length of the neck. In addition, a crescent of skin in the concavity immediately below the seventh or lowest cervical vertebrae is framed as a kind of obverse décolleté. The kimono wraps tightly up the front neckline. Other prominent fashion elements are placed to the back, including the larger motives of the kimono's pattern, the bow of the *obi*, and the knotted volume of hair embellished with combs. By shifting much of the visual interest to the posterior, the eye is necessarily drawn to look at the body from that perspective. This strategy is a reversal of the exposure of the neck, shoulders, and upper chest used in most Western fashion. But, whether attention is concentrated on the frontal poitrine or the posterior nape, the neckline and shoulders continue to be framed zones of exposure subject to aesthetic prejudice and erotic assessment.

Giovanni Boldini, *Conseulo Vanderbilt (1876–1964), Duchess of Marlborough, and Her Son, Lord Ivor Spencer-Churchill (1898–1956)*, oil on canvas, 1906. The Metropolitan Museum of Art, European Paintings, Gift of Consuelo Vanderbilt Balsan, 1946 (47.71)

Irving Penn, *Geisha, 1967*, 1967. Photograph: Copyright © 1970 by Condé Nast Publications Inc.

Maistres pleyns d'orgueil, ornons,
...ader voz bourses d'argent cherchons,
Why setten hier lobben op, al euen rep,
Alsoo lange alser gelt is in den lap.

Auecq ces fers chauds qu'on vous icy appreste,
En enfer puny seras, o layde beste.

Met dees yseren die ghy siet wermen
Sal ick v in helle noch doen kermen.

Auec ces fers en feu faisons ouurages,
Pour orner les laids & hideux visages.

Si de frases longues l'ornement me faille,
Auecq la bande pauure fauldra que ie m'en aille.

Krygh ick gheen lange lobben waer ick my wende
Soo moet ick dan loopen met cali's bende.

Les frases grandes que l'home viue
Au, col apres la vie monstre la mo.
Soo ick geleeft hebbe voor vrouwen en he
Moet ick nu als eenen gheest weder ke

Voicy mes frases i'apporte à empeser
Pour aux belles filles et femmes aggree
Om te behagen ionckvrouwen en wyuen

20   Overleaf: After Maarten de Vos, *The Pride of Women: Ruffs,* engraving, ca. 1600. The Metropolitan Museum of Art, The Costume Institute, Purchase, Irene Lewisohn Trust, 2001 (2001.341.2). Photograph: Mark Morosse, The Photograph Studio, The Metropolitan Museum of Art

Cornelis de Vos, *Portrait of a Woman,* oil on wood, 17th century. The Metropolitan Museum of Art, European Paintings, Marquand Collection, Gift of Henry G. Marquand, 1889 (89.15.37). Photograph: Peter Zeray, The Photograph Studio, The Metropolitan Museum of Art

Yoshiki Hishinuma, Evening ensemble, "Pêché Originel" collection, fall-winter 2001. Photograph: Firstview.com

The origin of the ruff is attributable to the wearing of white linen undergarments and shirts to protect the richer, more fragile outer fabrics of dress from both the perspiring body and the friction of the skin against the neckline and wrists. As witnessed even in very early depictions of this practice, the visible boundaries of undershirts and chemises were quickly ornamented by laces and embroideries. These embellishments were not only decorative but also functioned as reinforcing elements of the undergarment.

Amazingly, what began as the outlining of the neckline with ornamental edgings or small collars quickly evolved into a framing of the face. The ruff's discrete beginnings do not anticipate its accelerated inflation to shoulder-wide dimension. This broadening obliterated any exposure of the neck and consequently visually detached the head from the body. Additionally, the canting of the neckpiece created an optical illusion: the extended plane of white suggested a larger distance between the head and the torso. In effect, the ruff floated the head above the body at an ambiguous point that appeared farther than the physical reality.

The expense and ostentation of the ruff made it a compelling object of moral censure. As illustrated in the engraving on the overleaf, the stiffly starched collars typical of seventeenth-century black-suited burghers today evoke the probity and sobriety of bourgeois traditionalism. But at this height of florid fashionableness, the ruff conveyed the impression of an impulse to luxury and a submission to ludicrous vanity.

In Cornelis de Vos's portrait illustrated above left, the ruff's wide border of white obscures the neck and disrupts the relationship of head to body. There is a sense of disengagement of the head from the trunk. This spatial ambiguity introduces an optical attenuation. The linen cuffs in the portrait achieve a similar illusion; it is as if the sitter's arms were too long for her sleeves.

Yoshiki Hishinuma's ensemble shown above right extends the effect of the ruff onto the shoulders. Two rows of identically constructed bands adumbrate the puffed neckpiece. Although they are discontinuous, being open at center front, the two puffed rows at either shoulder create a visual segue to neckpiece and head. While Hishinuma's actual ruff is substantially smaller than the one depicted by de Vos, it functions with the ancillary bands to give the impression of a triple-tiered ruff that extends past the shoulders like the short mantles in vogue in the 1890s.

As illustrated above left, the costume of the Ndebele people of South Africa is another instance of the attenuating effect of a broad and wide neckpiece. Their neck rings, armlets, and leggings are constructed of rush and are then completely overbeaded. The lengthened impression is furthered by the drop of the neckpiece over the collarbone. The neck seems to originate at the base perimeter of the neck ring, thus optically extending the neck by at least two inches. The beaded rings are worn by young girls. They are removed at marriage and replaced by metal coils similar to those worn by Padaung women in Burma.

The designer Walter van Beirendonck is noted for his conceptually dense, visually provocative designs. In various collections, he has alluded to ethnic traditions, the murky perimeters of sexual fetish, and various subcultural expressions of youthful street fashions. The materials and technologies employed in his man's ensemble shown above right are without doubt contemporary. Yet the cumulative effect of his layering is atavistic and tribal. His neck ring has both the flaccid drape of a Polynesian warrior's feather *lei* and the deflated droop of a punctured inner tube. In any case, it is removed from the starched and structured propriety of a linen ruff. However, even in this enervated form, the ring continues to mediate the zone between the shoulders and the jaw in a similar way. Van Bierendonck further dissociated the head from the torso by pairing his neck ring with a turtleneck tunic that defines the neck. He then interrupts its connection to the body with a contrasting cape.

De Vos and Hishinuma, the Ndebele and van Beirendonck are participants in a shared optical strategy.

South Africa, Unmarried Ndebele girl wearing *cholwane,* 1976-82. Photograph: Natalie Knight Productions cc.

Walter van Beirendonck, Man's ensemble, "Dissections" collection, spring-summer 2000. Photograph: Firstview.com

21

The open ruff and the flat collar developed simultaneously with the circular ruff. They relied on a slightly different approach to the framing of the face and the suggestion of an attenuated neck. In the portrait by Frans Pourbus the Younger shown above left, the sitter wears a lace open ruff. Made of fine expensive lace or lace-edged linen, the open ruff is an ovoid that folds over on itself to form a double-layered horseshoe shape around the neck. Essentially, the lower layer supports the upper layer. The flat collar of similar effect is propped by a wire frame called a *supportasse*, or underpropper, to stand up in a canted halo around the whole head.

Unlike the ruff, the open ruff and the collar with *supportasse* could be worn with a deep V-neckline. This vertical fissure of exposed flesh begins at the sitter's face and continues down to the pit of the neck. As with the ruff at its widest, the broad open collar, by fanning over the shoulders, introduced an ambiguous relationship of head to torso. In the Pourbus portrait, stiff epaulets that wing out over the sleeves are used to support the impression of a longer neck. The epaulets are attached to the bodice at a slightly dropped angle and also extend the shoulder to a much lower point. The net effect is of the head poised at a greater remove from the torso.

The ensemble by Alexander McQueen seen above center tips up the horizontal plane of a lace collar to bracket the face. McQueen extended his neckline in a deep V to the base of the sternum. The effect is of the high-collared Directoire *Incroyables*, the dandies of that period, but the deep V-shape of the resulting neckline continues the strategy of the seventeenth century. Unlike these historical precedents, McQueen exposed the real shoulderline. The neck's optical extension is abetted by the upward flare of the collar. A high-necked lace dickey pulls the eye down and like the ruff, makes the head appear to float, disembodied from the neck.

McQueen's allusion to the 1790s Directoire period is more explicit in his design shown above right. During this period after the French Revolution, the *Incroyables* and their female counterparts, the *Merveilleuses*, took fashion to mannered extremes. As illustrated on the facing page, the silhouette of the day was extremely narrowed, with collars for men and ruffs for women raised to chin-obscuring heights. McQueen took the height of the *Incroyables'* rolled collar and pulled it upright. The jawline is covered, and even the tops of the ears are barely visible. The wing-like lapels part at center front to create a neckline that plunges to below the breasts. By submerging the wearer's head in the collar, McQueen introduced a sense of elongation, eliminating the conventional reference points of head to neck to shoulders.

Facing page: William Brocas, *Les Invisibles*, detail, hand-colored etching, published 1810 by T. Sidebotham. The Metropolitan Museum of Art, Drawings and Prints, Purchase, Harry G. Friedman Bequest, 1967 (67.539.60). Photograph: Mark Morosse, The Photograph Studio, The Metropolitan Museum of Art

Frans Pourbus the Younger, *Margherita Gonzaga*, detail, oil on canvas, 1625-30. The Metropolitan Museum of Art, European Paintings, Bequest of Collis P. Huntington, 1900 (25.110.21). Photograph: Peter Zeray, The Photograph Studio, The Metropolitan Museum of Art

Givenchy Haute Couture, fall-winter 1998, Ensemble with turned-up collar, designed by Alexander McQueen. Photograph: Bruno Pellerin

Alexander McQueen, Evening ensemble with high collar, "Dante" collection, fall-winter 1996. Photograph: Firstview.com

As seen on the facing page, Maasai women in the early twentieth century wore continuous coils of brass that create an effect similar to, if more visually permeable than the wide flat collars of seventeenth-century Europe. Both the brass coils and the planar collars of that period provide a foil for the head, and they also function as devices that block the view of the shoulders. In addition, the Maasai neck rings have a noticeably bib-like effect. Unlike the Pourbus portrait and the McQueen *Incroyables* discussed on the previous spread, in which the neckline in a tapering V introduced a vertical line to the ambiguously positioned head, the Maasai neck rings function exclusively on the principle of obscuring a clear view of the shoulderline. In that sense, the Maasai are conforming more closely to the effect and strategy of the seventeenth-century ruff. In all these cases, the shoulder plays an important role in suggesting the long neck through dress. Ironically, to achieve that attenuation, the neck itself is hidden almost as frequently as the shoulders. The camouflaged, elongated neck is conceptually reduced to the relationship of the head to the torso, so that the shoulders are inevitably implicated.

As seen above left, Junya Watanabe spiraled wires around his pleated top so that the coils control the shaping of the garment's neckline and shoulderline. With the vertical pleating, the garment fans at chin height in rigid pleating, stitched through and corralled by the wires. The fabric then opens up and arcs at either shoulder. The sleeveless armholes, splayed over an underdress, create a dropped shoulder line. The result is that the neck, completely hidden, appears to breach the distance between the raised neckline and the dropped shoulderline.

In his surrealist allusion shown above right, John Galliano sutured the broken frame of a disposable and collapsible umbrella with a raincoat. The articulated metal spokes support the high-necked collar that blooms open around the head. In this instance, the shoulders are not modified. Rather, the almost orthopedic structure of the metal spikes and the continued unfurling of fabric around the face introduce the same craning, chin-up posture imposed by neck braces. Like the small ruffs voguish in the Renaissance and the Directoire periods of the past, the subtly shifted balance of the head generates a lengthened neckline.

Facing page: Kenya, Africa, Maasai woman wearing neck coils, detail, ca. 1960s. Photographic postcard: S. Skulina, Pegasus Studio, Nairobi Kenya. The Metropolitan Museum of Art, Department of the Arts of Africa, Oceania, and the Americas, The Photograph Study Collection. Photograph: Mark Morosse, The Photograph Studio, The Metropolitan Museum of Art

Junya Watanabe, Pleated top ensemble, fall-winter 1998. Photograph: Giovanni Giannoni / *Women's Wear Daily*

Christian Dior Haute Couture, fall-winter 1989, Umbrella-neck raincoat, designed by John Galliano. Photograph: GAP JAPAN

26   Sudan, Africa, Dinka woman wearing neck corset, late 20th century. Photograph: Angela Fisher

Sudan, Africa, Dinka man wearing glass beads, late 20th century. Photograph: Angela Fisher

Isaac Snowman, *Portrait of Queen Alexandra,* oil on canvas, ca. 1902. Photograph: Courtesy of Wartski Ltd.

Facing page: Christian Dior Haute Couture, spring-summer 1997, *Rita* evening trouser ensemble, designed by John Galliano. Photograph: Firstview.com

The high-necked collar is a ubiquitous accent to a graceful neck. However, it alone cannot suggest a long line where none is in fact present. But for those who are naturally endowed, nothing establishes the focus on the neck and emphasizes its attenuation so effectively as a choker. For the Dinka people of the Sudan, choker-style necklaces like the one shown above left are laden with implications of status and wealth. However, it is evident in the construction of the pieces that there is also an aesthetic component related to the body. For both Dinka women and men, elements in the designs of the chokers point to a specific emphasis on the grace of the elongated neck. The Dinka necklaces are related to the beaded corsets and vests also worn in that culture. The necklaces have two wires that form a rigid center back spine to which the graduated strands of beads are attached. The spine of the necklace is also its closure. Like the wired spine of the corsets identified with the Dinka, the closure of the necklace extends beyond the part of the anatomy with which it is directly associated. Starting at the base of the cranium, it continues down past shoulder level to between the shoulder blades. A rear view of the necklace encourages the eye to read an exaggerated lengthening of the neck.

As exemplified above center, the necklace of the Dinka herdsman is similarly constructed and conveys an identical illusion from the front. In this case, a centered, contrasting line of beads establishes a vertical adumbration of the sternum. The choker of beads extending into a draped bib covering the nude body functions in reverse to the uncovered aperture of flesh in the plunging neckline in Western fashion. In both instances, it is the contrast to the rest of the body, uncovered or covered, that leads the eye to perceive a continuous verticality and attendant illusory length.

As shown in the portrait above right, Queen Alexandra of England popularized the fashion for chokers. Because of a scar on her neck, Alexandra invariably appeared in high collared fashions. For décolleté evening toilettes, she coordinated chokers with necklaces of varying length and covered her exposed neckline in a veil of precious stones.

Although it is an amalgamation of the royal jewels, Alexandra's parure is essentially the constitution of a high-necked bibbed collar similar to the fashion of the Dinka. John Galliano cited the extravagant jewelry of Queen Alexandra in his jeweled top on the facing page. He also referenced the beaded vests of Dinka women in a typical Galliano conflation of cultures and anachronistic juxtaposition. A chokered neck's elegant line is underscored when augmented by a cascade of matching necklaces.

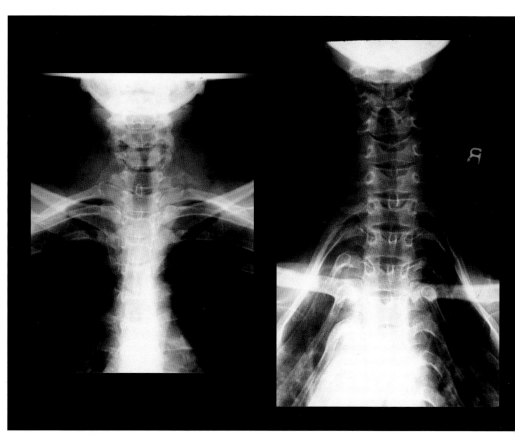

As illustrated on the facing page, the use of brass neck coils by the Padaung women of Burma is among the most extreme mechanisms for the creation of a longer neck. Padaung girls are fitted with the metal coils from the age of six. One piece with a counterweight at the spine widens over the collarbone. The other, a separate coil, is a cylinder that encases the neck. Since it is an anatomical impossibility for the vertebrae to be extended or stretched, the effect of attenuation is actually achieved by redirecting the collarbone. In most individuals, the collarbone angles slightly upward from a straight horizontal. By applying the weight of the neck coils, about eight pounds, the collarbone of the growing Padaung girl is deviated downward more than forty-five degrees. The mature longer neck, therefore, is actually a consequence of the extreme triangulation of the shoulder. This effect is evident in the X ray shown above right.

Recently, the style was in abeyance, since young girls are aware that the required shaping of heavy metal coils entails a lifetime of discomfort, and also since they no longer think the effect is modern. Significantly, the *New York Times* has reported that there is a countertrend emerging among the Padaung, precipitated by the economics of tourism. Because travelers will pay for photographs of Padaung women with the goose-necked look, Padaung men have begun pressuring their daughters to conform to the practice.

The photograph above left shows that the Ndebele of South Africa, like the Padaung of Burma, also utilize the weight of metal coils, which they call *zila*, to create the impression of a longer neck through the gradual collapsing of the shoulders. In the case of the Ndebele, girls are fitted with thick ornamentally beaded bolsters of rush, which crane the neck upward while pressing the shoulders downward. Upon marriage, the beaded rings are removed, and metal coils are substituted.

Facing page: Burma, Padaung woman with brass neck coils, ca. 1979. Photograph: Jorgen Bisch / NGS Image Collection

South Africa, *Portrait of Sophie Motha*, married Ndebele woman wearing a *zila*, 1994. Photograph: Mark Lewis

X rays showing the effects of Burmese neck coils on the skeleton, 1979. Photograph: Dr. John M. Keshishian / NGS Image Collection

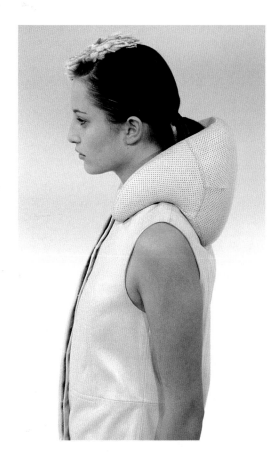

Cornelis de Vos, *Portrait of a Young Woman*, oil on canvas, 17th century. The Metropolitan Museum of Art, European Paintings, Purchase, 1871 (71.46)

Givenchy Haute Couture, fall-winter 1998, Coat ensemble, designed by Alexander McQueen. Photograph: Firstview.com

Hussein Chalayan, Dress with neck pillow, fall-winter 1999. Photograph: Firstview.com

Facing page: Kenya, Africa, Samburu girl wearing a nubility necklace stack, late 20th century. Photograph: Angela Fisher

The direct proximity of the neck to the face makes it an opportune zone for the display of wealth and symbols of luxury. In the needle arts, nothing was so prized as lace, and its initial discreet application to undershirts and chemises evolved into more ostentatious displays. By the seventeenth century, elaborately worked lace collars and cuffs were explicit and highly visible expressions of prestige. Because of the lavish expense they entailed, they were even subject to sumptuary laws, statutes instituted to regulate standards of dress.

The woman in the Cornelis de Vos portrait shown above left wears a Van Dyke collar. The broad field of lace seems to counter the contention that a triangulated shoulderline attenuates the neck, since in this instance, the neck is effectively submerged into the collar. In addition, the full sleeves of the period widened the shoulders. Because the collar began at the jawline and continued in a long slope to the visually lowered arms, the shoulder was not only optically extended but also triangulated. This angled, elongated, and lowered shoulderline appears to increase the distance between the head and shoulders, even as it shortens the neck. As exemplified above center, Alexander McQueen reprised this collar. With the more acute triangulation of his version, however, he increased the effect of a lengthened neck.

As shown above right, Hussein Chalayan recently mounted simple sheath dresses with padded neckrests. Ergonomically conceived, they introduced a triangulated line to the angle of the shoulder that functioned, in essence, in the same way as the Van Dyke collar and the beaded necklaces worn by the Samburu maiden illustrated on the facing page. The young women of the Samburu people in Kenya are considered marriageable only when they have accumulated a shoulderload of beaded necklaces from their male admirers. The thin bead strands are piled onto a beaded disc necklace similar to a style worn by Maasai women. Shoulder-wide, the disc supports a graduated stack that almost covers the chin of the Samburu girl. Since the triangulated pile of beads exaggerates the length of her neck, the Samburu girl's beauty accrues even as the evidence of her desirability accumulates and threatens to obscure her.

The eighteenth- and early-nineteenth-century shoulder was relatively level and narrow. The proper posture was to pull back the shoulders and thrust out the chest. By the end of the Empire period, however, the fashion for a new line had developed. The shoulder was pushed down rather than back and took on a sloping triangulated silhouette.

For all their variation, fashions from the late 1820s to the mid-1880s never deviated from the ideal of the rounded dropped shoulder. The visual consequence of this posture was the lengthening of the line of the neck. Without the aid of prostheses such as the eight-pound neck coils of the Ndebele and Padaung peoples, the fashionable woman who acceded to the authority of Paris was required to modify her anatomy through sheer willpower and physical discipline. From Ingres to Winterhalter to Tissot, the ideal neckline is documented in portraits of women, dressed and undressed.

The tyranny of the ideal was such that even Empress Elizabeth of Austria, famed for her health-consciousness and athleticism as well as her beauty, conformed to its standards. In Winterhalter's portrait on the facing page, she stands in profile. The painter depicted the extreme drop of his sitter's shoulder ambiguously. The off-the-shoulder neckline of her gown cuts across an unarticulated expanse of flesh. The line of her neck and shoulders is merged into a triangle, on which her head is perched.

The modification of a woman's shoulder stance was abetted somewhat by the corset. From the beginning of the 1830s onward, and with an increasingly complex structure, the corset was designed with lowered and widely splayed shoulder straps. Muslin underbodices that conform to that construction are visible through the sheer white cotton mull and organdy material of the two mid-nineteenth-century dresses shown above. Because the waistline is raised slightly to the lower ribcage, the pulled-down shoulderline creates a diamond-shaped torso, and the armhole is lowered almost to the level of the upper bust.

Facing page: Franz Xavier Winterhalter, *Elizabeth, Empress of Austria,* detail, oil on canvas, 1865. Photograph: Kunsthistoriches Museum, Wien oder KHM, Wien

Left: French, Wedding dress, ca. 1864. The Metropolitan Museum of Art, The Costume Institute, Gift of Mrs. James Sullivan, 1926 (26.250.2a-d). Right: American, Day dress, late 1850s-early 1860s. Courtesy of Museo de la Moda y Textil, Santiago, Chile. Photograph: Karin L. Willis, The Photograph Studio, The Metropolitan Museum of Art

Gavarn

Like the extended slope of the Van Dyke collar, the line of the 1830s shoulder was augmented in its angled effect by hugely inflated sleeves. To sustain such mass, a variety of supports were either worn as underpinnings or incorporated into the structure of the sleeves themselves. Examples of such sleeve supports are shown above left. Down-filled pillows were the most common, but chintz with ribs of wire or cane was also used to make somewhat airier, lantern-like forms.

When not sewn into the dresses, the sleeve supports were attached to the corset's shoulder straps by ties, as illustrated in the engraving on the facing page. These straps were oriented at a forty-five-degree angle from the body, and sometimes even more obliquely. In most instances, they fell beyond the juncture of the arm and shoulder and rested at the apex of the deltoid. Although impressive in mass, sleeve puffs did not disrupt the line of the shoulder. Instead, because they were poised so precariously on the upper arm, the sleeve's outline simply continued in a descending line from the shoulder. The engraving on the facing page also exemplifies the hairstyles of the day, with chignons pulled up from the nape of the neck in vertical loops. These styles emphasized the sloping shoulder even further by exposing the back of the neck completely.

The anachronistic conflations prized by designers with a post-modern sensibility are frequently of ironic intention. John Galliano created the Empire-style gown shown above right. Its sleeves resemble those of the late 1820s and 1830s. Galliano attached sleeve pillows of explicit artifice and structure to a historical fashion reputed to have been so lightly made that it revealed much of the natural body. But rather than following the modernist's impulse to express the integrity of structural elements, Galliano's intention appears to be more whimsical. His design exposes the fact that the ostensible naturalism of French Neoclassical rationality and Republican utopianism still shoulders the weight of fashion's caprice and ephemerality. Unlike the sleeves of the early Romantic period, the Galliano puffs extend the horizontal of the shoulder. They are so broad that they diminish the whole body, even the hips, to a more cylindrical effect. The attenuation of the neck is less affected than the narrowing of the body.

Facing page: Gavarni, *Le Corset,* engraving, 1835. Published in Louis Barthou, *Le Corset dans L'Art et Les Moeurs du XII au XX Siècle,* Paris, F. Libron, 1933. Photograph: Mark Morosse, The Photograph Studio, The Metropolitan Museum of Art

Four sleeve supports, The Metropolitan Museum of Art, The Costume Institute. Left to right: English, ca. 1828, Purchase, Irene Lewisohn Bequest, 1966 (CI 66.38.5b). American, ca. 1835, Museum Accession. American, ca. 1825. Gift of Mr. A. Hyatt Mayor. American, 1890s, Gift of Miss Jessie Rosenfeld, 1943 (CI 43.40.59a). Photograph: Karin L. Willis, The Photograph Studio, The Metropolitan Museum of Art

Givenchy Haute Couture, fall-winter 1996, *Joséphine* empire dress, designed by John Galliano. Photograph: Firstview.com

36 Left: American, Riding habit, ca. 1830.
Museum of The City of New York, Gift of
Mrs. Alexander G. Pendleton (50.328.1a,b).
Right: American, Bicycling jacket, 1893-95.
Block Island Historical Society Collection.
Photograph: Karin L. Willis, The Photograph
Studio, The Metropolitan Museum of Art

Jeremy Scott, Shrug ensemble,
"Contrepied" collection, fall-winter 1998.
Photograph: Firstview.com

Facing page: Viktor and Rolf, Dress with
puffed sleeves, "The Black Hole" collection,
fall-winter 2001. Photograph: Firstview.com

The early and mid-1890s saw a revival of the 1830s gigot, or leg-o'-mutton, sleeve. In both periods, the physical encumbrance of sleeve hoops and pillows did not preclude the adoption of the style for clothing intended for active sports. The rare *amazone*, or woman's riding habit, shown to the left in the illustration above left is an extraordinary example of the vogue for voluminous sleeves in the 1830s. Its sleeve-puffs are only slightly smaller in dimension than the bodice itself. Set low on a triangulated shoulder, they function as three-inch extensions of the shoulder.

The linen jacket from the 1890s shown above left to the right of the *amazone* is part of a summer bicycling ensemble. Three thin wire bands support the cap of each sleeve. They can be collapsed when the jacket is removed. The 1890s form of extending the shoulders while bracketing the shoulderline meant that the gigot sleeve was no longer intended to function primarily as an optical assist in the illusion of a lengthened neck. Even in the 1830s, the inflation of the sleeve had the equal if not more important purpose of diminishing the apparent size of the waist by contrast in scale. By the end of the century, this was the gigot sleeve's exclusive function.

As illustrated above right, Jeremy Scott, who is known for his sexually charged, highly theatrical style, has used the exaggerated shoulder to achieve the effect of a diminished waist and hips. In addition, the raglan-like juncture of bolero and dress creates the illusion of an attenuated neck. The angled neck-to-underarm contrast of the black puff-sleeved bolero and white sheath dress reintroduces the sense of a triangulated neckline. A similar strategy is accomplished in halter styles and sweetheart necklines.

In a very short time, the design team of Viktor and Rolf has created collections with an extraordinarily strong imprint. Their highly sculptural designs are often historically referential, with allusions to the eighteenth and nineteenth centuries; others are explicit explorations of the couture *metier*. In the example from their "Black Hole" collection on the facing page, the designers reprise the 1890s. Viktor and Rolf are noted for their manipulation of the proportions of the Grand Guignol effect. With their turgid gigot sleeves, they exaggerate the dimensions of a historical style that was itself an exaggeration of an earlier style. In doing so, they diminish not so much the waist as the whole of the torso.

Martin Margiela, Inside-out jacket, spring-summer 1997. Photograph: Ronald Stoops for STREET

Helmut Lang, Padded-shoulder dress, fall-winter 1999. Photograph: Firstview.com

Facing page: Gilbert Adrian, Suit, fall-winter 1945. Advertisement from *Vogue,* September 15, 1945

While the sloping shoulder has had a sustained if intermittent vogue, it was not until the late 1930s that a continuous broadened and level shoulderline was considered attractive on a woman. The enhanced shoulder was first popularized in the haute couture by Elsa Schiaparelli in the late 1930s. The innovation was possibly a response to the appearance earlier in the decade of an aggressively broad-shouldered silhouette in men's tailoring.

From a technical perspective, the padded shoulder was useful, since the extended shoulderline required an associated widening of the pattern piece, which in turn introduced more fabric to be draped over the bosom. On an aesthetic level, the broad shoulder created a V silhouette that appeared to narrow the hips. As early as the 1920s, the full and rounded hips and buttocks so evident until World War I had given way to a straightened hipline and flattened derriere. As it evolved from the late 1930s until 1947, the advent of Christian Dior's "New Look," the V shape of the ideal feminine form was increasingly exaggerated. As seen in the illustration on the facing page, the burgeoning shoulders and girdled shape of the period were epitomized by the American designer Gilbert Adrian.

Recently, Martin Margiela, famous for his conceptual approach to fashion, returned to the thinking that characterized his early collections. Faintly Dada and *arte povera,* these designs, exemplified above left, were described at the time as deconstructivist. If one attribute of deconstruction is the acknowledgment of the structural instability of any built form, then Margiela's dress-form piece might correspond. By referring to a mannequin, the surrogate body on which a garment is draped, the meaning of Margiela's jacket is transformed. No longer the basis on which a garment is measured to fit, it instead becomes a mechanism to reform and extend the body. On the other hand, it is modernist in its expression of structure as ornament, in its exposure of the black tapes that are references for the balanced grain of the fabric, and in the shoulder pads that regularize the curvilinear irregularities of the body.

In a somewhat related fashion, and with an equally humorous intention, Helmut Lang, whose minimalism often approaches an industrial brutalism, attached pads like military epaulets to the exterior of his fitted dress shown above right. Because the ovoid pads are not shaped like pads intended for garment-making purposes, the commentary is less about the techniques of dressmaking and tailoring than it is about the comic effect of another era's stylistic conventions.

In 1971, Yves Saint Laurent introduced a collection inspired by the 1940s, which is exemplified on the facing page. It was a statement in direct opposition to the narrow shouldered midi and maxi looks, which were being promoted by every other designer and major fashion publication at the time. It took almost a decade for fashion to revisit the padded shoulder, whether inspired by Saint Laurent's version or the styles of World War II.

However, from 1979 through the early 1990s, padded shoulders were *de rigueur*, especially for tailored clothing. By the early 1980s, at the point of the most massive shoulderlines, even designers who advocated a body-conscious functionalism, like Giorgio Armani and Donna Karan, employed football-player-scaled shoulder pads. Pads of that date were more closely related to the dramatic and fantastical designs seen in forties movies than they were to actual street styles of that decade. So endemic and exaggerated was the "football" shoulder in men's and women's fashion that one critic asked, with a reference to a fashion folly of the previous decade: "Are shoulder pads the bell bottoms of the 1980s?" In fact only in the 1990s was the shoulder pad decade finally supplanted by a revival of 1970s fashions, with their tight fit, high-cut armholes, and narrow shoulders.

When the wide shoulder has reappeared more recently, it seems to be primarily in designs of highly theatrical effect. Over the past two decades, Yohji Yamamoto has moved from aggressively avant-gardist designs to collections that express both a consciousness of the past and a studious, if irreverent interpretation of its forms. His fur coat shown above left cites outerwear from the 1890s. The model walked down the runway with her hands holding the front of her coat together, further eliciting associations to the bent elbow cut of dolmans from that period.

Alexander McQueen's coat seen above right alludes not to the past but to other cultures. The metal neck rings and feather headdress point to Africa, where, in the rituals of certain men's secret societies and the exceptional female secret society of the Mende culture, dancers perform with masks bordered by thick camouflaging skirts of grass. For his coat McQueen dispensed with the mask but kept the effect of the massive body-obscuring grass cover.

Facing page: Yves Saint Laurent, Fox coat, spring-summer 1971. Photograph: Hans Feurer

Yohji Yamamoto, Peaked-shoulder fur coat, fall-winter 1996. Photograph: The Fashion Group International Archives

Givenchy Haute Couture, fall-winter 1997, Coat, designed by Alexander McQueen. Photograph: Firstview.com

Thierry Mugler, Jacket, 1988. Photograph:
Courtesy of Thierry Mugler Archives

Facing page: Pierre Cardin, Man's suit,
"Superman" collection, spring-summer
1971. Photograph: Cardin Archive

In the 1930s, much before Elsa Schiaparelli's adoption of the look for women, men's suits were seen to initiate the expansion of the shoulderline. Christian Dior's "New Look" of 1947 all but eradicated the padded shoulder from womenswear, although the style did persist in modified form in men's tailoring, as a straightening, rather than an extending, of the shoulderline. But it was not until the late 1970s that the broad shoulder returned to the forefront of fashion. Then, the "power shoulder" appeared simultaneously in both men's and women's fashions.

Pierre Cardin was an early advocate of the stylized and broadened shoulder. From the beginning of his career, Cardin imbued a discernibly sculptural quality to the cut of his designs. He was one of the first designers to successfully present and market both menswear and womenswear collections. Cardin's influence on menswear was formidable: the Mod jackets affected by The Beatles were inspired by his more expensive Continental creations. The sleek, almost space-age modernity of his tailoring was very much in sync with the 1960s. A decade later, the subtle sci-fi aspects of Cardin's collections had evolved into more dramatic and stylized expressions. In his "Superman" suit, shown on the facing page, all the proportions of the day are kept intact, except for the exaggerated upsweep of the extended shoulder. The mild-mannered Clark Kent suit is suddenly invested with the breadth of the DC Comics superhero's identity, and with a V-shaped tapering torso.

While Cardin, an *éminence grise* of French fashion, was exploring the possibilities of the shoulderline with swagger, younger designers like Thierry Mugler and Claude Montana were also endorsing the new silhouette. Of the two, Mugler, especially, conflated 1930s Social Realism, DC and Marvel Comics, and art moderne for a specifically futuristic effect. Mugler is a noted photographer and specializes in juxtaposing his designs against heroic architectural monuments. This is well exemplified in the illustration above, in which the Chrysler Building is a backdrop for his broad-shouldered superwoman.

As shown on the facing page, the flaring epaulets of Thai dancers are a distinctive elaboration on the theme of the extended shoulder. Curving upward at its terminus like the pagoda roofline from which it takes its name, the pagoda shoulder is heavily stiffened and rigid. Unlike inflated gigot sleeves or shoulder-padded garments, the pagoda shoulder was not incorporated into the structure of the sleeve or the body of the garment.

In his ensemble shown above left, Alexander McQueen torqued the sticks of wooden fans into a bolero. Merging *koi*, or carp, imagery from Japanese painting with a pan-Asian coolie hat and the pagoda shoulder, the designer suggested an almost Gilbert and Sullivan assembly of skewed stereotypes. However, while known for his provocative persona and politicized creative vision, McQueen appears less interested here in addressing cultural bias than in exploring picturesque forms in the way of eighteenth- and nineteenth-century Orientalists. In this view, the East is neither a cultural nor a political reality. Instead, it is an imaginary construct. The ensemble is recognizably Asian, yet without any sources in the real world.

The pagoda shoulder takes another form in Thierry Mugler's velvet suit shown above center. Mugler has a penchant for the arcing seam and the crescent cut. In this interpretation of the look of Thai dancers, he applied his extraordinary tailoring skills to the construction of the curving shoulder and sleeve cap. McQueen's pagoda shoulder jacket, illustrated above right, is similarly constructed. McQueen used a detail from *The Crucified Thief*, a painting of about 1410 attributed to Robert Campin. His choice of the bad thief freights the design with tortured meaning. Angled in a V by the weight of his crucified body, the thief's arms mime the lift of the jacket's shoulders.

Yves Saint Laurent's 1980 "Pagoda" evening suit is illustrated on the following two pages. In this conflation of Eastern and Western imagery, Saint Laurent took the oak-leaf motif of Napoleonic dress uniforms and merged it with the Orientalist curl of the pagoda shoulder. Like costumes from Broadway and Hollywood productions of *The King and I*, Saint Laurent's interpretation of dress from the court of the King of Siam is a romantic fiction—a transposition of time, culture, and gender.

Facing page: Thailand, *Herorama* costumes, 1947. Photograph: W. Robert Moore/NGS Image Collection

Givenchy Haute Couture, spring-summer 1998, *Hiroshise* [sic] ensemble, designed by Alexander McQueen. Photograph: Bruno Pellerin

Thierry Mugler, *La Tonkinoise* suit, spring-summer 1997. Photograph: Patrice Stable

Alexander McQueen, Jacket, "It's a Jungle Out There" collection, fall-winter 1997. Photograph: Firstview.com

Overleaf: Yves Saint Laurent, *Pagode* evening suit, spring-summer 1980. Photograph: David Bailey

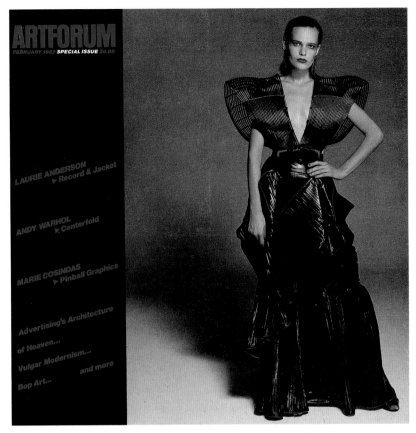

Christian Dior Haute Couture, fall-winter
2001, Kimono coat, designed by John
Galliano. Photograph: Firstview.com

Issey Miyake, Evening ensemble with rattan
top, spring-summer 1982. Photograph:
© ArtForum, February 1982

Facing page: Artist unknown, Japanese
school, Samurai wearing formal kimono,
1860s-90s. The Metropolitan Museum of
Art, Photographs, Gift of H. de Rassloff,
1918 (1994.129). Photograph: Mark
Morosse, The Photograph Studio, The
Metropolitan Museum of Art

The aversion to shaped pattern pieces that can be seen in much regional dress sometimes results in a broad shoulder without shaping. This occurs when the essentially two-dimensional garments are pulled or wrapped over the body. However, in Japanese male formal attire, such as that seen in the photograph on the facing page, a *kamishimo*, a jumper with wide wings, is deliberately folded into form over the shoulders and worn with a matching *hakama*, a stiff trouser-like overskirt. The result is a masculinized breadth that contrasts with the round shouldered effect of everyday kimonos, which are made of softer materials.

Throughout his career, Issey Miyake, a master at complex origami-like constructions, has also explored the making of body covers with unconventional materials and techniques. As exemplified above right, Miyake draped pleated and glazed garments over a lacquered bamboo framework in an extraordinary series of samurai-inspired ensembles. The cage can be seen as an extrapolation of the *kamishimo*. The designer has sought techniques in both artisanal trades and advanced technologies. In this case, he worked with the maker of lacquered bamboo implements for the *chano-yu*, or tea ceremony. Despite the traditional source for its form and making, the final effect, as in all Miyake's work, is so insistently avant-gardist that it warranted the cover of *ArtForum*.

With its surprising synthesis of sources, John Galliano's work can take on an almost hallucinatory logic. In his Kabuki-inspired outfit shown above left, the pattern of a Japanese *noshi*, a traditional bow-like offering of bundled streamers, is enlarged into a facsimile of a formal man's kimono. The *noshi* is tipped on its side, its knotted center becoming the waist of Galliano's ensemble and the variegated streamers fanning out to form an approximation of a *kamishimo* and *hakama*. A famous Japanese kimono, a *furisode* with a *noshi* pattern, is designated as one of the country's "important cultural properties." Galliano has taken that important and auspicious motif and informed it with the lurid animation and neon-inflected sensibility of contemporary Japanese "anime."

CHEST

Hans Holbein the Younger, *Jane Seymour,*
detail, oil on oakwood, 1536.
Kunsthistorisches Museum, Vienna.
Photograph: Copyright Erich Lessing /
Art Resource, New York

52

French School, *Gabrielle d'Estrées in her
Bath,* detail, oil on canvas, 17th century.
Photograph: Musée Conde, Chantilly,
France / Giraudon / Bridgeman Art Library

Overleaf: Jean Paul Gaultier, Evening gown,
"Geishas in Technicolor" collection, spring-
summer 1999. Photograph: Firstview.com

The history of the chest is as much about its suppression as it is about its augmentation. The mid-fourteenth century produced body-conscious styles and fitted cuts accomplished through shaped pattern pieces. Now, contouring seams that acknowledged the bust's swell, as well as the fanning gathers accommodating fullness that had been seen previously, configured the fashionable bodice. In either case, the breasts were evident, if not emphasized.

In the sixteenth century, the vogue for boned bodices, called bodies, transformed the torso of a woman of style into an inverted cone shape. A dramatic denial of any of the bust's natural contours occurred. Paintings and sculptures of this period show that the construction of the bodices did not generally concede the presence of the breasts. This subduing of the torso's natural curvature in the Renaissance period can be seen in Holbein's portrait of Jane Seymour, illustrated at the upper left, in which the décolleté is represented by a trapezoidal expanse without apparent contours. The flattened upper swell of the severely constrained bosom was depicted only infrequently, as if the complete absence of the breasts were the preferred standard of beauty. This was partly the consequence of a focus on other areas of emphasis—the neck and shoulders, or more prominently, the waist and hips. But even the concise shape of the breasts depicted on nude figures suggests a preference for smaller busts rather than the more prominent and pendant forms associated with wet nurses and maturity. Cleavage and mounds that swelled too prominently above the neckline were not desirable.

It is difficult to understand this obliteration of the bust, which happened as a result of the reshaping of the body's trunk into the clean geometry imposed by the corset. Obviously, the volume of the bust had to be shifted, but apparently not upward, since that would divulge an excessive pulchritude. Given pictorial evidence, it is likely that the shift was lateral and accommodated by the corset's widening flare from waist to apex of chest.

Fashion historian Anne Hollander has argued that in art of the period, even the nude is depicted with all the characteristics of deformation dependent on fashionable dress of its time. Representations in Renaissance-period nudes, then, can be thought of as a corporeal mapping of the shifting to the sides of the chest that the corset or structured bodice imposes. A study of the positioning of the breasts on nudes reveals both their often widely separated placement on the chest and the discrete volume of the desired smallish form that is a requisite of the final look of the dressed body. In the depiction of Gabrielle d'Estrées with her wet nurse in the background, shown at the lower left, the discrete and widely spaced aesthetic breasts of the period beauty are juxtaposed with the large functional breasts of her servant.

However, the mid-seventeenth century brought the advent of a new ideal. As represented by the fuller more robust figures seen in Dutch paintings of the period, deep cleavage was presented as an attractive attribute for the first time. Before this, large, full, and pendant breasts were associated with the lower social classes. They elicited such undesirable associations as old age, coarseness, vulgarity, moral turpitude, and even witchcraft. Now, overflowing bosoms, a consequence of the binding of well-endowed bodies, were depicted with a wholesome ruddiness and an aspect of domesticated bourgeois bounty evidenced in Ruben's portrait of Suzanne Fourment at the upper right. Even the rippling surfaces of nudes proposed an aesthetic that reveled in the earthbound and the material. For the Dutch painter of the time, signs of the ephemeral nature of the corporeal appear only to substantiate the beauties and richness of life and its pleasures.

In the eighteenth century, the globular forms and deeply creased cleavage seen in the hearty bustline of seventeenth-century Dutch beauties reverted to the smaller apple-like form that was more typically and consistently admired. For almost the next two hundred years, the small firm bust was reasserted as the paradigm of beauty and nubility. Sometimes, in the eighteenth century, a transparent veiling of a light mull-fabric *fichu,* or triangular scarf, obscured the nipples, which appeared above the topline of both the corset and the chemise. More typically, the aesthetically normative bust, despite the crush of the corset, was betrayed only as a slightly heaving undulation at its open neckline. In the late-eighteenth-century, during France's Directoire period, the bust was for the first time not treated as a marginalized adjunct to the corset's engineering of the waist. Although chemise gowns had waistlines raised to the underbust, they were thought to introduce an ostensibly "natural" body, and they rejected any rigid underpinnings, or at least avoided the impression of any reliance on them. As an increasing focal point, the bust became the object of strategies independent of the waist for its optimum display. The lightly boned and cord-quilted corsets that replaced earlier carapace-like models are notable for introducing gussets, inserts that support each breast independently. The intentions became support, separation, and accentuation.

From the end of the eighteenth to the beginning of the twentieth century, the bosom was enhanced by corsetry rather than pressed to the sides and obscured. Still, the reigning mode was to have the exposed décolleté appear more softly undulating than ample with creased cleavage. The bust was expressed but not exaggerated to an artificial well-endowed dimension. Still, by the last quarter of the nineteenth century, corsets were sometimes designed with pads for the bust's underside to create the fleshier rounded look prized in the Belle Epoque.

The unbroken line of the bosom, a neckline without the creasing of cleavage, found a kind of apogee at the turn of the twentieth century. The monobosom was the result of a straight front corset with a lowered topline. The bosom was cradled, and the resulting effect was a lowered apex, a pigeon-like breast. This look persisted from 1900 to World War I. In 1914, Caresse Crosby, an American socialite, received a patent for a halter for the bust originally created out of ribbon and two handkerchiefs. Earlier brassieres of various forms had preceded her invention, but it is Crosby's design that has come to be thought of as the first bra. However, this technical innovation had little opportunity to evolve, at least for another decade. The 1920s were dominated by the straight-as-a-board silhouette that was a signature of the *garçonne*, or flapper. Unlike previous eras of fashionable bust-suppression, 1920s bandeau bras were independent costume elements that addressed the breasts directly. Although they appeared to be unshaped, small darts gave them a shallow three-dimensionality. Their main function, however, was to bind rather than accommodate the bust. The bandeaus of chiffon, satin, or lace relied more on the suppleness of their materials than on any elements of shaping for comfort.

In the decade following, the innovation of the bias cut contributed as never before to an articulation of the body through the dress. To avoid the appearance of undergarments in unsightly relief, women—especially in eveningwear—sometimes abjured them completely. Fashion in this period encouraged an unfettered bust, even as it conformed to and was accompanied by a modish slimness.

By the end of the 1930s, the availability of new elastic materials precipitated the design of a corset with a defined bust. Because it was not a period that viewed the large bustline as desirable, brassieres had been developed to aid in the support, or lift, and reconfiguration of the bigger bosom. Other innovations immediately preceding World War II included the strapless bra and the panty girdle, designs that would become staples of the undergarment industry by the 1950s. These new designs were motivated by the fact that foundation garments allow a greater number of people with their varied natural attributes to conform to an ideal of beauty. Both the technology and the structure of these bras were the primary influences on the period that followed.

During World War II, shortages of and restrictions on materials precluded a dissemination of many of the developing stylistic changes of the late 1930s. But from the period immediately following the war until the mid-1960s, the geometrically abstracted cone-shaped breast became the norm in Western high fashion. Cleavage was increasingly aspired to, and the consequence was a bra design that lifted the breasts and also pushed them together. The most unnatural effect of the cone bra was that it centered on its apex, the nipple. The result was an almost totally supported breast with none of the gravitational effects of a natural bustline. As seen in the highly naturalistic depiction by Graham shown at the lower right, most women's breasts, unless very small and youthful, are characterized by a longer slacking upper slope and a fuller rounder undercurve. By configuring the bust into an idealized shape, the conical bra was also defying the inevitable pull of age.

By the end of the 1960s, a new androgynous aesthetic had emerged. The feminist movement took on the bra as a symbol of patriarchal societal constraints. In the immediate post-war era, the dramatically endowed woman was not precluded from stylishness. But the 1960s emphasis on the lithe and willowy silhouette of youth caused a certain aesthetic disjunction. While fashion pursued a path that endorsed the linear ectomorphy of high fashion models, the erotic imagination continued to prize the large breasted woman. A large bust and cleavage, then, was situated in a peculiarly ambiguous aesthetic predicament: even as it was unfashionable, it was seen as provocative and desirable.

As the most obvious secondary sexual characteristic of women and as a zone of some malleability, the bust has been the site of major physical manipulation. Whether suppressed by corsets in sixteenth-century Europe, deformed into a single mass in the early twentieth century, or padded, propped, and protuberant in the 1950s, even the small and apple-like breasts that have been the most persistently fashionable are not spared the "improvements" of dress. Other areas of the body have manifested more extreme transformations over time, but it is the bust that has witnessed the most varied structural interventions in the twentieth century.

Peter Paul Rubens, *Portrait of Suzanne Fourment ('Le Chapeau de Paille')*, detail, oil on oak, probably 1622–25. National Gallery, London. Photograph: Copyright Erich Lessing / Art Resource, New York

Robert Graham, *Elisa*, detail, bronze, 1993. Courtesy of the artist. Photograph: Malcolm Lubliner

In the late eighteenth century, corsets were cut with an increasingly lower neckline. In addition to constricting the waist, they also began to support and enhance the volume of the bosom. The emphasis on the breasts was a deliberate rather than an ancillary effect of the corset's displacement of flesh. This can be seen in the introduction to the corset's construction of gussets, inserted at the chest to support the breasts separately. In earlier examples, the bust had been accommodated by an increase in circumference at the corset's conical flaring at the neckline. But this schematized construction of the corset's parts served to contain and obliterate the actual shape of the breasts, despite the structural acknowledgment. The caricature reproduced above left demonstrates that by the 1790s, a more explicit suggestion of a woman's true anatomy was introduced, in corsets that created the smoothly undulating double swell at the chest that characterizes the *belle poitrine* of the period.

Because dress up until the time of the French Revolution was heavily boned with stiffened undergarments, even figures that did not conform to the ideal, willowy proportions of the period found some corrective assistance through the structure of their constraints. As seen in Gérard's portrait of Madame Récamier, reproduced on the facing page, the Directoire and Empire periods, from the 1790s to the 1810s, were characterized by fashions that held little refuge for women of more ample proportions. Still, for all the apparent revelation of the natural body suggested by the sheer Neoclassical styles in vogue at this time, similar, if somewhat less constructed technical strategies were utilized to create the newly fashionable high-bosomed silhouette.

It was not until the mid-twentieth century that the lift of the bosom was also used to express the spherical distinction of each breast. At their most extreme, conical shaping, underpads, and wiring created an effect of breasts that were both enlarged and "lifted" to the point where they were symmetrical in their torpedo-like profile. Consider the instance of the Playboy Bunny ensemble, illustrated above right. The reconfiguration of the natural bosom by the satin encasement of this uniform is so explicit in its artifice and abstraction that the bust approaches the eroticized dissociation of a fetish.

Facing page: François Pascal Simon Gérard, *Madame Récamier,* 1803. Musée Carnavalet, Paris. Photograph: Giraudon / Art Resource, New York

H. Humphrey, *Patent bolsters,* 1791. Published in Nora Waugh, *Corsets and Crinolines,* London, B.T. Batsford Ltd., 1954. Photograph: Mark Morosse, The Photograph Studio, The Metropolitan Museum of Art

Playboy Bunny ensembles, worn by *Playboy* magazine Playmates of the Year at opening of Hugo Boss store. Left: Jodi Ann Paterson (2000). Center: Brande Roderick (2001). Right: Heather Kozar (1999). Photograph: Marion Curtis/DMI/Timepix

Le Bon Genre, No. 5, La Toilette, detail, lithograph, ca. 1801, published in *Le Bon Genre: Reimpression des 115 Gravures Publiées Sous Ce Titre de 1801 à 1822*, Paris, Boulevard Montmartre, 1928. Photograph: Mark Morosse, The Photograph Studio, The Metropolitan Museum of Art

Issey Miyake, Bustier, fall-winter 2000. Photograph: Firstview.com

The unencumbered and explicitly revealed body that was the ideal of Neoclassical dress was widely subject to writers' and caricaturists' moralizing pen and acerbic critique. Invariably, the targets were vanity and the foolish excesses of fashion. As evidenced in the illustration reproduced above left, nowhere was the obsessive follower of *la mode* more pointedly the object of ridicule than when a woman embraced a trend so wholeheartedly as to don falsies. Here, the bust enhancer is not simply a padded filler; it also accedes to the requirements for naturalism under the sheer materials of the day. This prosthesis is anatomically descriptive to the last detail. The sculpted nipples are even realistically colored. In 1799, *The Times* of London reported that modish women in transparent gowns were enhancing their natural attributes with artificial ones. In an article often quoted by contemporary fashion historians, it was noted: "The fashion of false bosoms has at least this utility, that it compels our fashionable fair to wear something."

In total contrast, Issey Miyake insulated the breasts with a buffer of pile-lined felt in the ensemble shown above right. Perhaps he was reacting to the erotic objectification ultimately expressed by similar contemporary latex renderings that are sold as sexual paraphernalia. Maybe he was also responding to the fetishistic isolation of the bust as a primary erogenous zone in Western culture. Worn with shoulder straps like a sandwich board, Miyake's breast covering is a relief of slanted ovals with no suggestion of nipples. It is so schematic that it gives no hint at pectoral muscle or mammary tissue. Unlike the caricatured early-nineteenth-century *femme-du-monde* falsies, where the intention was naturalistic anatomical enhancement, the Miyake stiff fabric bust pad, worn outside the dress, acts as armorial breastplate. Additionally, Miyake's protective bib evokes a censor's blackout rectangle. Even more than a bulletproof vest, it is a shield from the male gaze.

Since the late 1960s, with its celebration of youth and unisex effects, a new paradigm for the fashionable breast has emerged. During the post-World War II era, the large bust was prized, but post-feminist period breasts depend less on size for their erotic allure. Instead, they rely on the ability to disclose the details of their form, especially the nipples. Massive geometricized conical shapes gave way to smaller but more explicitly anatomical shapes. The nipples suggested the absence of a bra, and their visibility set off an erotic trigger. Ironically, the articulated nipple as an erotic sign in fashion was a consequence of feminism. Brassieres, with their reformative abstraction of the natural bust, were an apt symbol for early feminists' repudiation of the cultural

control of the female body. By burning the bra, it could be argued, women situated their bodies on par with those of men. By casting off the control of bras, what some social critics have called women's eroticized, commercialized, and politicized breasts might alternatively be equated with the neutral "natural" breasts of many non-Western cultures. However, the real physical and visual consequence of the freed bust was something else. The relief of the nipples became more discernible under garments made of light knits or supple wovens, and the absence of the rigid supports of the brassiere resulted in a newly apparent movement. In addition, gravity pulled the braless breast into a more pendant asymmetrical profile, with a long, faintly concave upper breast line and a shorter, more distinctively convex under-breast line.

Yves Saint Laurent is among the earliest designers to expose the breasts by showing transparent tops on braless models. Like Rudi Gernreich, the innovative American designer of the 1965 topless bathing suit, Saint Laurent used mannequins who were only modestly endowed, creating a less erotically charged effect. In 1969, however, Saint Laurent created a series of neoclassical gowns. As exemplified above left, they were fitted with gilded body castings by the sculptor Claude Lalanne. The allusion to armor was explicit, as was the reference to the poetic surrealism that typifies Lalanne's work. The bodice's molded form, with its "from life" naturalism on the body, became itself more rigid than the unnatural configurations of any of the bras discarded earlier by feminists. Tom Ford, mining the Saint Laurent oeuvre, designed the molded leather bustier seen above right. He emphasized the nipples by elaborating on the relief of their aureoli and by minimizing the bust. The nipples, one with a rhinestone piercing, are thereby made the carrier of gender and sexual content even more explicitly. Ford also reasserted the centered conical symmetry of the idealized breast.

Yves Saint Laurent Haute Couture, Evening ensemble with bust mold by Claude Lalanne, fall-winter 1969. Photograph: Duane Michals

Yves Saint Laurent Prêt-à-Porter, spring-summer 2001, Evening ensemble with bustier, designed by Tom Ford. Photograph: Firstview.com

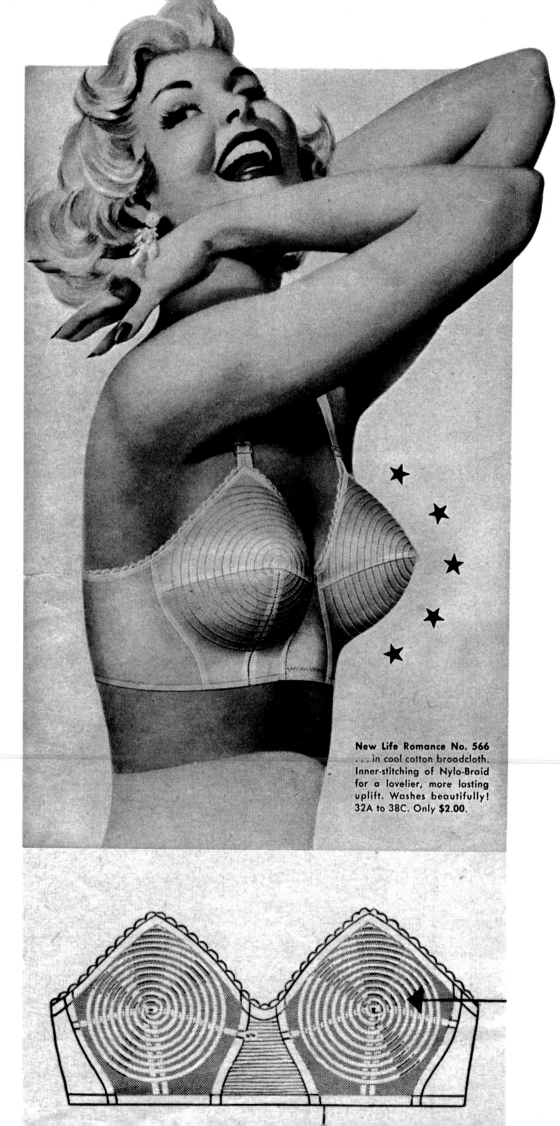

New Life Romance No. 566
. . . in cool cotton broadcloth.
Inner-stitching of Nylo-Braid
for a lovelier, more lasting
uplift. Washes beautifully!
32A to 38C. Only $2.00.

A number of technical innovations in materials took place in the 1930s and 1940s, including man-made fibers and durable elastics. These new possibilities coincided with the fashion world's impulse to shape the bust. The rapid shift from the bust suppression of the 1920s to the unencumbered and pendant bosom of the 1930s was immediately followed by a dramatic introduction of brassieres with structured support.

Then, in the post-World War II period, the ability to stitch bra cups in a spiraling whirlpool configuration resulted in the torpedo-like shapes exemplified by the advertisement on the facing page. The bust was made at once relatively inert, stiff, and geometrically regular. This encasement of the breasts, however, did not mute their erotic charge. Instead, the projectile effect, with deepened cleavage, created an almost lurid focus. As exemplified above right, the brassiere was now so structured that it retained the imprint of the body even in its absence. Like the corset, the glove, or the shoe, it emerged as an increasingly common object of fetishistic reference.

Rei Kawakubo is known for her provocative aesthetics; she often deliberately seeks beauty in what is seen by convention as taboo. In her ensemble of 2001 for Comme des Garçons shown above left, Kawakubo overlaid a trenchcoat with an underwire brassiere made of wool worsted. While other designers have cited the detailing and forms of intimate apparel, this strategy of underwear as outerwear is essentially and almost unavoidably prurient at some level. While Kawakubo generally disavows any explicit narratives applied to her work, a brassiere worn outermost in a series of layers inevitably foregrounds the issue of gender. However, while Kawakubo references a garment from the period of the bust's most highly eroticized focus, she cites its least provocative form, the long-line bra and fashions it in a fabric that by convention situates it as outerwear.

The long-line with its wide corselet perimeter was intended to provide greater support for women with larger breasts. The result is paradoxical: the detailing in bras for women who were naturally endowed, the ostensible period ideal, was more orthopedic than sexy. As a result, this silhouette introduces a functional reading to the cone-shaped cups generally freighted with sexist implication. They are support and protective encasement rather than idealized and eroticized attributes of feminine identity.

Facing page: Spiral-stitched cone bra, "New Life Romance" advertisement, 1940s. Photograph: The Advertising Archives

Comme des Garçons, fall-winter 2001, Trenchcoat ensemble, designed by Rei Kawakubo. Photograph: Firstview.com

Left: American, *3-D* by Splendor Form, 1950s. Center: American, *Beau-Bra,* late 1940s-early 1950s. Right: American, *Delightform,* 1950s. Photograph: Karin L. Willis, The Photograph Studio, The Metropolitan Museum of Art

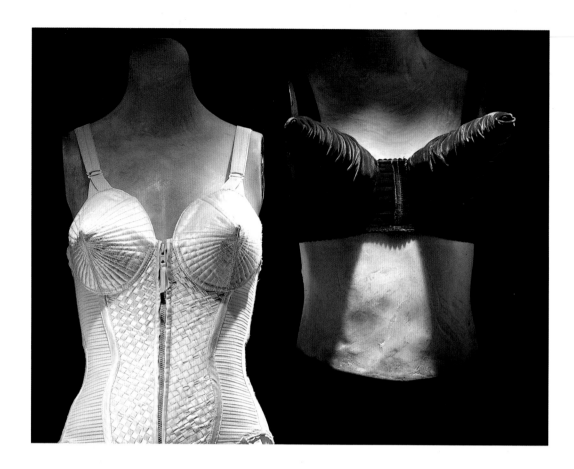

The notion of a corset with separately constructed bust cups is a phenomenon of the late
twentieth century. In the past, the preference for neck- and bustlines without a creased cleavage
resulted in a lateral displacement of the breasts. Even during periods when the breasts were
treated individually, as in the early and mid-nineteenth century, the body of the corset tended
to bifurcate the bust, flattening the apex of the breast as it also provided support.

The general adoption of the bullet-shaped bra cup after World War II coincided with
the return of the waist cincher, a light corselet. With Christian Dior's Belle Epoque revival of
the wasp-waisted silhouette, corsetieres contrived new waist-suppressing underpinnings with
attached brassieres. More than any nineteenth-century model, this undergarment, the bra-girdle,
is the prime source of Jean Paul Gaultier's signature corset.

As exemplified above, the reintroduction of the corset to a post-feminist generation
was abetted by Madonna. The iconic rock diva wore several versions of Gaultier's corset looks.
Madonna's advocacy of faintly archaistic, intentionally provocative underwear as exhibitionistic
outerwear coincided with the evolving feminist theory espoused by such writers as Camille
Paglia. Madonna's exuberantly sexualized persona suggested that an explicit control of one's
image might transform, or at least destabilize, the patriarchal relationship of voyeuristic male
and sexually objectified female. After Madonna, to be the object of the male gaze was not
necessarily to be subject to it.

Madonna's collaboration with Gaultier for her "Blonde Ambition" tour introduced
further complexities to the paradoxical concept of the empowered boy toy. In her corseted
allusion to blonde starlets of the 1950s, Madonna surrounded herself with a supporting cast of
lithely muscled male attendants endowed with aggressively conical artificial breasts. The male
dancer's donning of the breasts was not remotely convincing as a transgender act. Their
masculinity is never compromised. Nevertheless, these fake breasts communicate a potent
ambiguity. They push gender-bending beyond the typically subtle nuances of androgyny to an
almost comical clash of hypertrophic male and female elements. As seen on the facing page,
Gaultier had introduced similar breasts before, in his 1984 collection. The cockeyed lunacy of
their caricatured form reveals the designer's humorous intent and impulse for parody.

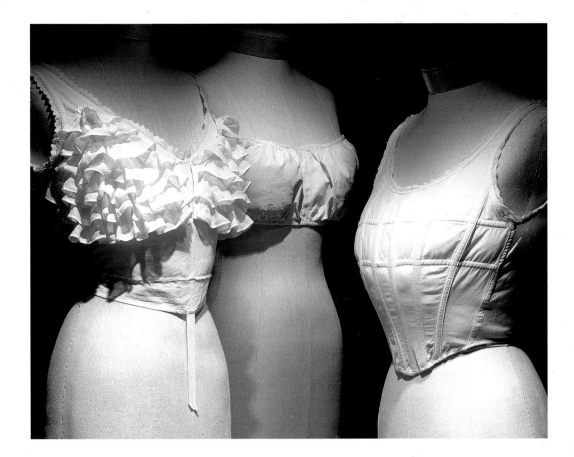

John Singer Sargent's painting reproduced on the facing page shows the pigeon-breasted silhouette called the monobosom. This wide, well-padded expanse was the preferred ideal that lasted for a few brief years at the beginning of the twentieth century. It persisted in diminished form until World War I. The massive pouch-like shape was a consequence of the lowered topline of the corset. The breasts were allowed to hang freely, so that their apex, if it had been possible to discern (it was not), would appear to fall near the base of the sternum. Pulchritude was the effect essentially sought, but with no disclosure of the natural form of the breasts. Even in very décolleté evening gowns, cleavage was not desirable.

An enormously inventive array of prostheses and shape-makers survive from this period. They serve as evidence of the lengths to which women went to create this generous unarticulated bosom. For the woman less than well-endowed, chemisettes, or underbodices, with button-on ruffled bust enhancers, like the one illustrated above left, were intended to fill out the silhouette softly. The ruffled attachments were situated on the inside of the chemisette, which was cut to the preferred fuller shape. In this way, the woman was assured of a smooth and unbroken line.

A more direct but less elegant solution was the fitting of pads over the natural bust. In most instances, the prostheses are rather discreet, but as in the example shown above center, a wide bandeau was sometimes filled with two large circles of horsehair. The dispersal of the stuffing in this particular configuration underscores the nature of the desired effect: the padding gave each breast a broader circumference and a more ambiguous outline. With the hollow of the cleavage filled, the breasts would merge into a voluminous unified entity.

However, even women with substantial breasts could not simply allow them to be supported without some modification, since any suggestion of the separation of the breasts or their individual form was to be avoided. Lightly constructed boned chemisettes like the one shown above right reshaped the bust into the desired pigeon-like effect of the monobosom.

Facing page: John Singer Sargent, *Nancy Astor*, detail, oil on canvas, 1906. Photograph: National Trust Photographic Library / John Hammond

Left: American, Chemisette with detachable ruffles (shown inside-out), 1910-14. The Museum at the Fashion Institute of Technology, New York, Museum Purchase (P82.1.12). Center: American, Bust enhancer, ca. 1900. The Museum at the Fashion Institute of Technology, New York, Gift of Mrs. Benjamin Hinkley Riggs (69.221.1). Right: American, Chemisette, ca. 1903. The Metropolitan Museum of Art, The Costume Institute, Purchase, Hoechst Fiber Industries Fund, 1982 (1982.316.8). Photograph: Karin L. Willis, The Photograph Studio, The Metropolitan Museum of Art

Pneumatic Bust Forms

Perfected under Late "H. & H." Patents

"Light as air," cool, healthful, durable; give unequaled style, grace, comfort, and the admirable and superb proportions of the ideal figure. So perfect and natural are they that dressmakers fit gowns over them and never know by sight or touch that they are artificial. Women of refinement everywhere welcome them as a relief from the old unsightly and unhealthy contrivances. Worn with or without corsets, fit any figure, adapt themselves to every movement "as a part of oneself." A grateful support to mothers. In bathing they can't be detached, buoy the wearer and make swimming easy.

Write for photo-illustrated circulars and convincing testimonials.

All correspondence and goods mailed under plain seal without advertising marks.

ADDRESS

**Henderson & Henderson
Dept. B6, Buffalo, N.Y.**

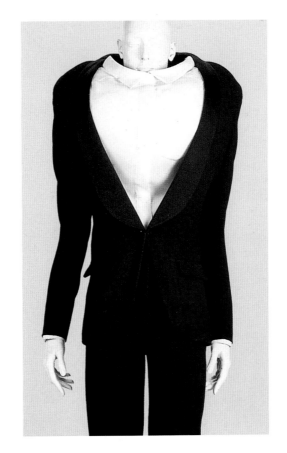

Très Secrète *
(VERY SECRET)

INFLATABLE BRA

MAKES ALL OTHER WAYS TO A LOVELY <u>NATURAL</u> BUSTLINE OLD-FASHIONED!

A. ADJUST

B. INSERT TUBE—INFLATE   C. PRESS TO SEAL

Patented and Pat. Pending in U. S. A. and Foreign Countries.

*Reg. U. S. Pat. Off.

Secret Satisfaction That Only The Finest Can Give

Très Secrète is your secret! It's the only bra ever made that gives you the desired bust-line! No heavy pads or rubber cups—just weight-less air for that lovely figure you've always wanted. Très Secrète, with two removable plastic, adjustable inflatables, is made of long-lasting figured nylon. (Quick-drying, needs no ironing!) You don't need a try-on—just come in and buy one! In black and white—sizes 32, 34, 36 A and B cup. $5.00

LA RESISTA CORSET COMPANY
45 Park Avenue, New York City, N. Y. • Bridgeport, Conn.

After the late-nineteenth-century invention of rubber and canvas air bladders for applications as varied as inner tubes and water wings, it was only a matter of time before the technology was used to address the underdeveloped chest. Pneumatic bust forms such as those in the advertisement reproduced on the facing page are an early example of fashion's ingenious marshalling of science to the service of beauty. The use of such an apparently drastic beauty aid is not unreasonable if the reigning silhouette of the day, the monobosom, is considered. With its high-necked coverage and puffed front, the monobosomed gown could even camouflage a full-torso inflatable form.

The idea for a pneumatic bust enhancer was revisited in the 1950s. By that time, the air pockets were isolated in separate bust cups, as opposed to the earlier monobosom version, which relied on a single pocket of air to create the effect of one broad bosom. The profile of the breasts also changed significantly. The stylish form of the 1950s was no longer soft and rounded. Instead, each breast was high and sharply pointed. A straw was required to control the size and firmness of the "adjustable inflatables" of the *Très Secrète* bra, seen in the 1952 advertisement reproduced above left.

Viktor and Rolf have proposed contemporary variants on the monobosom silhouette. Common metaphors for breasts—pillows, clouds, balloons—are suggested by their 1998 tuxedo ensemble, shown above right. In this creation, the model is transformed into an inverted bowling pin, with a ballooning torso that narrows over the hips and legs. The crisp white shirt, more Lewis Carroll fantasy than Gibson Girl monobosom, is so puffed with tulle that it appears to consume the model's head. The ensemble's exaggerated distension, however, is only a slightly more satirical representation of actual mechanisms intended to facilitate the long-standing impulse to pump up the bust.

Facing page: Henderson & Henderson, "Pneumatic Bust Forms," advertisement, published in *The Delineator,* September 1903. Photograph: Mark Morosse, The Photograph Studio, The Metropolitan Museum of Art

La Resista Corset Company, *"Très Secrète Inflatable Bra,"* advertisement, published in *Mademoiselle,* February 1952. Photograph: Mark Morosse, The Photograph Studio, The Metropolitan Museum of Art

Viktor and Rolf, *Atomic Bomb* tuxedo suit, fall-winter 1998. Photograph: Peter Tahl for the Groninger Museum, The Netherlands

The *Air Up* bra, shown on the facing page, introduced a more contemporary profile by shaping the bust as spherical rather than conical. Still, elements of the 1950s brassiere were retained in this post-feminist reaction. By placing the air pockets so that they bracket the underside of the bra, the breasts are pushed up and together. The resulting shape appears to repudiate gravity and the natural slope of the bust, and to create a deeper cleavage. The structural mechanisms operative in the *Air Up* bra are similar to those used in the Playboy Bunny uniform. In effect, breasts in an *Air Up* bra present an image as artificial as the torpedo shapes formed by the heavily quilted cups of the past.

 The ideal of a full chest has not been restricted to women. Men's tailored clothing has often featured felted padding across the upper chest. In addition, men's corsets in the eighteenth and nineteenth centuries abetted the impression of a barrel chest by displacing some flesh upward. But it was mostly the optical effect of a contrastive small waist that actually emphasized the male chest's expanse.

 In 2001, Issey Miyake designed the men's outfit shown above left. It has the proportions of a football player in his padded uniform. Air pockets function as inflatable pectorals. In the blow-up jacket from his 1997 men's ensemble seen above right, Walter van Beirendonck played with a similar idea, but he positioned his low-tech air valves as prominent nipples. Both designers provide the opportunity for an exaggerated musculature. But on the runway, van Beirendonck's pneumatic musculature was not inflated to maximum capacity. By this choice, the designer deflated the very superhero masculinity that he invoked.

Facing page: Gossard, *Ultrabra Airotic* (*Air Up* bra), spring-summer 2001. Photograph: Courtesy of Gossard

Issey Miyake, Man's shorts ensemble, spring-summer 2001. Photograph: Firstview.com

W.&L.T. (Wild and Lethal Trash), Walter van Beirendonck, Inflatable jacket ensemble, "Avatar" collection, fall-winter 1997. Photograph: Firstview.com

In the planar dresses that characterize both 1920s fashion and regional costume traditions, allure is created by emphasizing richness of fabric rather than by shaping the garment. As exemplified in the 1926 jacket shown on the facing page, the forms of the individual breasts were virtually eliminated, at least in high fashion. Elasticized corsets were required to accomplish the unbroken fall of cloth across the bodies of women with voluptuous figures. They often extended from above the breasts to the hips. Those of more fashionably modest endowment could rely on bandeau bras, which only faintly acknowledged the swell of the breasts. Cut almost flat, bands of chiffon and lace provided virtually no support and functioned primarily as suppressors.

The breast is arguably the most prominent secondary sexual characteristic of the female body. Given this factor, its eroticization and the exaggerated extension of its contours would seem to be inevitable. However, in most cultures and in most eras, breasts have not had the obsessive somewhat fetishistic focus that characterizes our time. On the other hand, examples of the active suppression of the bustline are equally rare. In addition to the corsets worn during the late Renaissance and early Baroque periods, only one other period, the 1920s, can also be seen as a time when breasts were aggressively physically repressed. Some ancient images of women with lengths of breast-binding fabrics show a similar intent to eliminate the contours of the bust, but it is far more typical to find examples of breasts exposed and unconstrained or clearly depicted under body-revealing draperies.

Examples from the Far East suggest breast-binding practices. However, closer examination reveals that the effects are actually the result of building up the waist rather than binding and flattening the bustline. Consider the costume of Bali, as exemplified by the three sisters in the photograph above left. Here, the bust is visually diminished by the thickly wrapped waist. Because the waist is built up, the prominence and distinction of the breasts are virtually eliminated, giving the whole figure a simplified almost cylindrical geometry. Even in Japan, where a cylindrical form is also prized, the breasts are allowed to express themselves above the tightly wrapped *obi*, or decorative sash. However, when John Galliano sourced the components of the Japanese kimono in the wool and lacquered straw dress of 1996 shown above right, he raised the traditional *obi* to cover and bind the bust.

Facing page: Baron Adolph de Meyer, "Rose-Colored Velvet Jacket-Goupy," published in *Harper's Bazaar,* July 1926. Photograph: Mark Morosse, The Photograph Studio, The Metropolitan Museum of Art

Three Balinese sisters in festival dress, 1912-14. Photograph: Gregor Krause, reprinted from *Bali,* 1922

Givenchy Haute Couture, *Winter Ascot* collection, fall-winter 1996, Dress, designed by John Galliano. Photograph: Firstview.com

WAIST

Greek, Hellenistic, *The Venus de Milo*,
marble, ca. 100 B.C. Musée du Louvre,
Paris. Photograph: D. Arnaudet /
J. Schormans, Copyright Réunion des
Musées Nationaux / Art Resource,
New York

Hugo van der Goes, *The Fall, Adam and
Eve Tempted by the Snake,* panel from
the diptych *The Fall of Man and The
Lamentation,* detail, oil on oakwood, ca.
1470. Kunsthistorisches Museum, Vienna.
Photograph: Copyright Erich Lessing /
Art Resource, New York

Overleaf: Thierry Mugler, *Chimère* evening
ensemble, fall-winter 1997. Photograph:
Patrice Stable

No zone of a woman's body has been more subject to visual and physical adjustment than the waist. Even in the loose draperies of Classical antiquity, the waist was acknowledged by the blouson. However, it was not until the advent of more body conforming clothing in fourteenth-century Western Europe that the cycle of the migrating waist was initiated. From 1350 onward, even the idealized waist of the Venus de Milo, seen at the upper left, manifested a broadness that was to be anathema to the fashionable ideal.

In late Medieval and early Renaissance examples, the waist either fell low on the hipbones and was identified by a decorative girdle or was cinched high under the bust. In the first instance, the torso's shape, including the waist's indentation, was visible, but the acknowledgment of the aesthetic waistline was determined by the garment's belt.

When Christian Dior declared, "Without foundations, there is no fashion," he was not overstating the importance of corsets in historical transformations of style. Although the body's area of greatest malleability is between the lowest rib and the crest of the pelvis, the corset's influence on its reshaping reaches beyond these parameters. With an extended upper part, the corset can reform the ribcage, suppress or express the bust, and accommodate or displace the flesh under the arms and the back. Lengthened downward, the corset may reshape the hipline and flatten or round the abdomen. In almost every case, it transforms the wearer's posture and carriage.

The earliest corsets as we know them originated in either Spain or Italy in the first half of the sixteenth century. Their antecedents appear to have been unboned cloth underbodices. The earliest corsets, called bodies or stays, laced close, with a distinction made between those with a front (open) or back (closed) lacing. The most important structuring stay, called a busk, was placed at front center. Created of wood, metal, whalebone, or horn, the busk introduced a rigid line down the corset's front. More complicated contours, in which the center frontline of the corset curved out over the abdomen, could be achieved by bending metal or by heat molding whalebone and horn into the desired shape. From the beginning, it became apparent that the corset was not simply about diminishing the waist. It also subjected the whole torso, including the abdomen, to an idealized geometrical transformation. To that end, its bottom edge might dip in front, in back, or both. And the smallest dimension might not be at the corset's base point but rather might hover above it.

If the fashioned waistline is defined as the narrowest point of the torso, it was transient even at the earliest phases of its development. As exemplified in the depiction of Eve at the lower left, the waist of a fifteenth-century beauty might be located at her tenth rib, below her sternum but above the actual zone of fleshiness. On the other hand, a Tudor aristocrat's waist was pushed down to the point of her pelvic crest. The effect on the upper ribcage could be pronounced. In some portraits, the sitter's chest is shaped like an inverted cone, with the ribcage pulled in on the sides into a form that would appear almost circular in cross section. Other images describe torsos as rigorously V-shaped though broader, suggesting that their final configuration was not as dependent on the transformation of the ribcage for effect.

Portraits from the sixteenth century, the beginning of the adaptation of the corset, show a slight bagging of fabric beneath the bust. This may be evidence that the corset was still somewhat supple overall, that there were not as many bones in the original corsets, and that corsets were not as compressive as they were to become by the end of the sixteenth century. By the seventeenth century, there was little deviation from the strict and smoothed contours established by the corset and therefore almost no evidence of the body's natural form. Corsets were rigorously abstracted, and the breasts, midriff indentation, and stomach were made to conform to an unarticulated V.

In addition to creating a straightened posture, the more rigid corset with a front-center busk required the wearer to bend not at the waist but at the hips, thus predicating her movements. This ramrod posture, which inspired courtly manner and carriage, persists to this day in activities as varied as fencing, dressage, and some forms of dance. The deportment of the body was inextricably tied to the Renaissance belief in physical control as evidence of moral and social rectitude. Constraining a woman's body and movements was also inevitably associated with her ability to express her sexual nature. A popular conceit of the eighteenth century was the image of a woman pulling out her busk as a weapon against the advances of an aggressive suitor. The gesture was fraught with ambiguities. By drawing out her main "stay," the embattled subject removed the primary physical and symbolic impediment to her virtue. The busk, which was often embellished with love imagery or amorous poetic conceits, is interpreted less as an object of castigation and resistance than as one of provocation and inducement.

The beginning of the nineteenth century brought the advent of lighter Neoclassical fashions with raised below-the-bust waistlines. Corsets were much less constructed than they were earlier. Because the empire waistline actually girded the ribcage, corsets did not have to constrict the midriff as aggressively. But paradoxically, they covered a much larger zone of the torso than they had before. Often made of cotton sateen, they were given structure by corded quilting, a long busk, and more elaborately sectioned pattern pieces. They also noticeably lacked the overall stiffened shaping that resulted from past use of layered buckram and sized or starched canvas. For the first time, the corset's structure acknowledged that the bust was composed of two separate breasts. Cord quilting and simple quilting-reinforced side panels restrained the waist. A three-to-five-inch wide zone described an almost cylindrical midriff. The lower skirt of the corset spread over the abdomen. It flattened the stomach but indicated the hips. Because the lacing closure was at the back of the corset and was generally more loosely tied as it spread below the waist, the expression of the derriere was given some latitude.

Gaston Lachaise, *Standing Woman*, bronze, 1927. The Metropolitan Museum of Art, Modern Art, Bequest of Scofield Thayer, 1982 (1984.433.34)

In the 1840s, an attenuated tapered waist came back into vogue. The side waistline of the fashionable bodice rested on the upper hipbone and extended in a point over the abdomen. Corsets began to return to greater construction and boning to achieve the new silhouette. Reinvested with elements of earlier designs, the new corsets were the most tectonically sophisticated to date. Like other technological and production advances of the Industrial Revolution, the corset can be seen as a wonder of nineteenth-century engineering. As the structural complexity of the corset advanced, so too did its shape. By mid-century, the corset's form underwent an almost continual decade to decade transformation. The 1850s and 1860s saw the curious elevation of the waist to the lower ribcage. Although the ribcage cannot accommodate the kind of dramatic cinching possible in the malleable midriff, the level of the lower ribs is not subject to the fluctuations of weight possible in the fleshier parts of the abdomen. Therefore, locating the waist there provides a measurement that is stable, though not the smallest one achievable. By the 1870s, a deliberately rounded stomach was preferred. Typically, shaping was accompanied by a technological advance, for example the curve of the spoon busk. The corset also controlled the relationship between the expression of the abdomen and the bust. The relatively natural laterally flattened ribcage of the 1830s to 1860s began to deepen into the rounded shape imposed by the hourglass form of the 1870s and 1880s.

The late nineteenth century was generally characterized by a waist that appeared very small from both the front and rear views but widened in the side view. Although the waist was constricted all around, angled panel pieces and boning pressed it in more at the sides. Because the back to front width was not altered by the dynamics of this cinching, its unadulterated dimension appeared broader compared to the dramatic narrowing of the front and back. This curious illusion of a widened waist in side view was addressed by the beginning of the twentieth century. The upper torso expanded, resulting in the dramatic effect of a waist pinched in all around. In addition, the new corset introduced an S-shape to the spine by thrusting the lower chest forward and the buttocks backward. The whole corset was shifted down so that its topline barely supported the bust and its hipline extended over the whole of the abdomen. The shaping of the body before World War I is exemplified by the work of Gaston Lachaise, whose nudes, as shown at the upper right, continue the pre-war aesthetic, even in a period of its fashionable demise. In the decade preceding World War I, an apparent easing of the strictures of the waist took place. The couturier Paul Poiret, with his designs inspired by the Orient and the Directoire, was said to have liberated women, at least those fashionably svelte, from their corsets. Poiret's columnar silhouette supplanted the wasp-waist. However, since an overall slimming of the body was required, a more encompassing, though more supple, corset was introduced. In a curious paradox, this torso-wrapping corset persisted through the 1920s, a period noted for its lack of a defined waist. Because the flapper look was based on a shapeless androgyny, women of curvaceous form now had to repress the contours of their waists and also of their busts and hips.

"Singer Britney Spears, wearing nude-color two piece outfit, performing at the MTV Video Music Awards," September 7, 2000. Photograph: David Cameron / Zuma / Timepix

During the next two decades, girdling focused on the hips. An exception was the 1939 Mainbocher corset, which attempted to renew interest in the laced waistline. Its influence was precluded by the cataclysmic disruptions of World War II, and the hips continued as the primary zone for reduction until the severely cinched waist returned with Christian Dior's 1947 "New Look" collection. The "New Look" cinches and the corseted looks of the 1950s were the last uniform embrace of the wasp-waisted look in Western fashion.

As witnessed by celebrities like Britney Spears, seen at the lower right, the waist must now be perfectly physically toned to accommodate the low-rise, navel exposing styles presently in vogue. Adjustment of this zone with the aid of corsetry is no longer possible. Today, the natural body can achieve the prevailing standard of aesthetic beauty through diet, exercise, and most drastically, surgical intervention.

Examples of metal corset forms from the sixteenth century survive in a number of collections. It is thought that they served an orthopedic function. In addition to the rare authentic forms, a number of examples exist that appear to date from the nineteenth century. The specialized interest in such eccentric manifestations of body reformation was extensive enough, apparently, to create a market for such objects.

The metal corset shown on the facing page is thought to be one such nineteenth-century example, made for a collector's cabinet. Its inside waist measurement is fifteen inches, but this seemingly impossibly small dimension is not the evidence that precludes the corset's authenticity. In fact, an American riding habit from about 1830, shown in chapter one, has a similar side-seam measurement and a sixteen-inch waist. Rather, a nineteenth-century fabrication is suggested by the regularity of the triangular cutouts that form the zigzag pattern of the corset, together with the curved and pointed shapers that extend over the stomach and buttocks.

The publication of such examples has inspired some contemporary designs. Shown above left is Alexander McQueen's gilded leather corselet over a pantsuit. Its triangular perforations mime the ironsmith's openwork pattern. Rendered in metal, the decorative perforations would have served to lighten the weight of the corset. In leather, the lace-like eyelets introduce a greater suppleness. As illustrated above right, McQueen was even more explicit in his reference to archaic forms of corsetry in his 1997 collection. The line of buckle closures down the center front alludes to the metal strap and pin fasteners of metal corsets and also to the mechanisms for securing classical breastplates and more contemporary straitjackets. These multiple references, including some with dark implications, are typical of the historical and politicized themes that inform McQueen's work.

Facing page: European, Metal corset, thought to be from the 19th century in the style of the 16th century. The Museum at the Fashion Institute of Technology, New York, Gift of Janet and David Desmon (87.94.3). Photograph: Karin L. Willis, The Photograph Studio, The Metropolitan Museum of Art

Givenchy Haute Couture, spring-summer 1999, Pantsuit with corselet, designed by Alexander McQueen. Photograph: Firstview.com

Givenchy Haute Couture, spring-summer 1997, Trouser ensemble, designed by Alexander McQueen. Photograph: Firstview.com

Issey Miyake, Wire bustier, 1983.
Photograph: Daniel Jouanneau

Alexander McQueen, *Cossack* ensemble
with silver wire top by Shaun Leane,
"The Overlook" collection, fall-winter 1999.
Photograph: Firstview.com

Facing page: Junko Koshino, *Bustier in
Synthetic Codes* ensemble, fall-winter 1992.
Photograph: Koshino Junko Design Office
Co., Ltd.

The imagery of the caged waist and torso engineered into an ideal shape is a persistent one. While the orthopedic early metal corsets were more closely associated in their design to armor than to tailored dress, metal, with its strength and surprising flexibility when properly formed, made its appearance in the busk, spine, and boning of later corset designs.

But unlike its prior application as perforated iron or steel sheets or thin flattened sticks inserted into channels of quilting-stiffened fabric, the recent use of metal has relied on wire to reframe the human form. Issey Miyake has explored a number of industrial techniques to create dress that conforms to and reforms the body without reliance on traditional tailoring or textiles. In his design shown above left, he resorted to a wire cuff to shape the waist. Miyake, who is known for his subtle humor and interest in punning words and forms, contained a feathered garment in this wire cage.

In his ensemble shown above right, Alexander McQueen in collaboration with the jeweler Shaun Leane, created a tightly fitted carapace to which the torso is forced to conform. Like the prosthetic metal corsets of the sixteenth century, the McQueen piece controls more than the flesh; because of its high neck, short "sleeves," and extension to the upper hipline, it also circumscribes the body's movements. While the designer calls the piece his *Cossack* top, it has less to do with loose full-sleeved asymmetrical overblouses than it does with the stiff hieratic imagery in Russian Orthodox icons.

As illustrated in her ensemble shown on the facing page, Junko Koshino took an architectural approach by cantilevering a contoured wire form. This piece grips the torso at the sides. Rather than defining the body by constriction, Koshino's design projects her idealized contours forward and expands the torso's dimensions. This strategy has also been employed by such designers as Cristobal Balenciaga, who believed that capacious garments larger than the body convey the sense of a smaller figure. In the Koshino garment, the black silhouette of the real body shape is screened by the bustier's white wires, which resemble the contour lines of topographic mapping. The ability to see the body paradoxically emphasizes the illusion of its reduction.

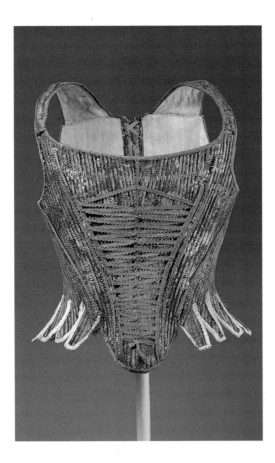

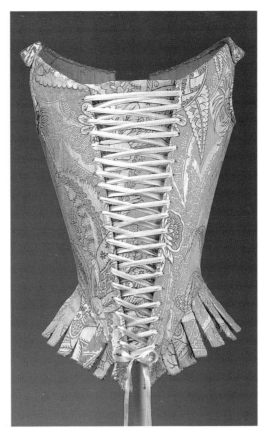

The eighteenth-century corset was generally either in two major parts with lacing at center front and back or in one piece with a center back closing. The Thomas Rowlandson caricature on the facing page illustrates the strenuous application of force required to achieve the most body-minimizing fit. It is a humorous fantasy, not in its depiction of the difficulty of tight lacing but rather in the actual mechanisms of lacing.

It was most common to introduce the long lace through an eyelet at the waist, feed it in a upward zigzag skipping every other opening, and then loop it across the top to zigzag back down to the waist. In this way, the greatest pressure applied to the two loose ends would occur where it was most desired, at the waist. As exemplified above left, the French corset, with its functional back lacing, trompe l'oeil laced front, and false stomacher, is evidence of the most common technique of lacing. So too is the contemporary threaded lacing of the Italian two-part corset seen above right.

Because there was a significant pulling in of the waist, a tabbed peplum accommodated not only the hips but also the displaced flesh. Although the waist was the primary focus of the corset's transformation of the body, the contiguous zones of chest and hips were necessarily implicated. In the eighteenth century, the shoulders-back posture, together with the corset's more-or-less conical configuration, caused the ribcage to narrow and deepen. As the ribs were pressed in on the sides, they were pushed out in front. The chest in cross-section resembled a rounded triangle and the waist a deep oval. This look contrasts radically with our contemporary torsos, which tend to have a laterally ovoid or elliptical form.

To accomplish this transformation of the waist and chest, the corset had to be almost armor-like in its structure, despite its richly brocaded silk covering. With its rigid form of whalebone and layers of canvas, the corset reconfigured the body's flesh and bones.

Facing page: Thomas Rowlandson, "A Little Tighter," hand-colored etching, published by S. W. Fores, May 18, 1791. The Metropolitan Museum of Art, Drawings and Prints, Elisha Whittelsey Collection, Elisha Whittelsey Fund, 1959 (59.533.429). Photograph: Mark Morosse, The Photograph Studio, The Metropolitan Museum of Art

French, Silk corset, 1750-74. The Metropolitan Museum of Art, The Costume Institute, Gift of William Martine Weaver, 1950 (CI 50.8.2). Photograph: Karin L. Willis, The Photograph Studio, The Metropolitan Museum of Art

Italian, Silk corset, 1770s. The Metropolitan Museum of Art, The Costume Institute, Gift of The Metropolitan Museum of Art, 1940 (CI 40.173.6 c-e). Photograph: Karin L. Willis, The Photograph Studio, The Metropolitan Museum of Art

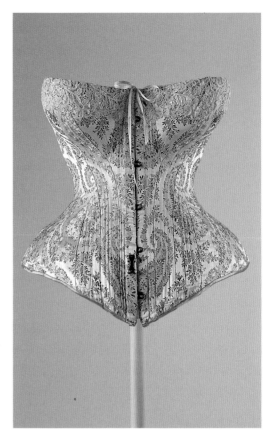

Honoré Daumier, *Emotions Parisiennes,*
"C'est Unique! J'ai Pris Quatre
Tailles,"detail, hand-colored lithograph,
published in *Charivari,* February 7, 1840.
The Metropolitan Museum of Art, Drawings
and Prints, Elisha Whittelsey Collection,
Elisha Whittelsey Fund, 1962 (62.650.258)

French, Silk corset, 1891. The Metropolitan
Museum of Art, The Costume Institute, Gift
of Miss Marion Hague, 1945 (CI 45.27).
Photograph: Karin L. Willis, The Photograph
Studio, The Metropolitan Museum of Art

Facing page: James Jacques Joseph Tissot,
The Gallery of HMS Calcutta (Portsmouth),
detail, oil on canvas, ca. 1876. Photograph:
Tate Gallery, London / Art Resource,
New York

In the nineteenth century, corset design witnessed a transformation in structure and shaping at an unprecedented pace. In Honoré Daumier's 1840 lithograph shown above left, a slightly pot-bellied gentleman exclaims, "This is unique! I've possessed four shapes." The corsets in the window act as souvenirs of the bodies of his mistresses.

The 1840s corset tended to a long, tapered midriff, coincident with the faintly gothicizing attenuation of the torso that was the favored standard of feminine beauty at the time. Daumier's print depicts the squatter bulging forms more characteristic of the 1830s. His portrayal suggests a lag in the perception of men about *la mode*'s accelerated transformation of the ideals of beauty—even a man such as Daumier, who documented contemporary life.

By mid-century, the complexity of the construction of corsets was such that prizes were awarded at international expositions for innovations in their designs along with those of crinoline hoops and bustles. At their most inventive, these types of fashion infrastructure were forms of engineering and fell under the protection of technical and scientific patents.

In the absence of a bustle, the wasp waist of 1876 to 1887 created an hourglass or mermaid-like silhouette. With the exception of the emphatically diminished waist, a softly rounded female form was preferred. The eighteenth-century busk, a straight wooden or metal rod that went into the center front channel of the one-piece corset, was replaced by a hooking steel pin-and-eyelet closure that curved over the belly. The profile of the fashionable woman was curvaceous from every angle, and a rounded belly balanced the swell of the bust above the waist.

In James Tissot's painting of the modish bourgeoisie, reproduced on the facing page, the transparency of the back of the sheer mull gown *à la Sirène* worn by the woman in the foreground reveals the low topline of her corset. At the front, therefore, the bust was not pushed up—as in the Empire style—so much as cradled. With the lower bust stance and the curvature over the stomach, the net effect was of a compression of the distance between bust and hips as in the example shown above right.

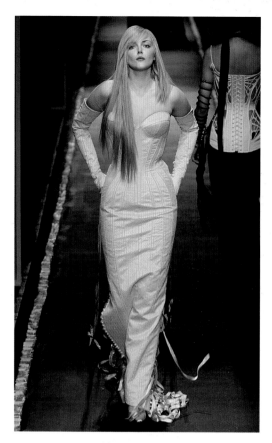

Front and back views: Jean Paul Gaultier Haute Couture, *Botte Secrète* evening gown, "Des Robes qui se Dérobent" collection, spring-summer 2001. Photograph: Firstview.com

Facing page: Jacques Fath, Evening gown, spring 1947. The Metropolitan Museum of Art, The Costume Institute, Gift of Richard Martin, 1993 (1993.55). Photograph: Neil Selkirk

Corsets were often constructed of rich materials and opulently trimmed. There was, however, no apparent convention related to color or pattern until after World War I. Although elaborate brocades and heavy silk-satins were often used for fancier corsets, plain cotton and linen examples were more common. By the 1920s, corsets in a limited palette of ivory, black, or pink were most popular. And by the 1930s, certain shades of dusty-pink silk-satin were so consistently seen in lingerie that the fabric in that hue evoked immediate associations with feminine intimate apparel.

In Jacques Fath's glamorous evening gown, shown on the facing page, the piecing and boning of the corset-bodice appear like *pentimenti* on its surface. The designer exploited shell-pink satin and its association to the boudoir by merging the construction of a nineteenth-century corset and its back lacing with the liquid drape of pre-World War II fashions. The color of the satin and the faint archaism of its lacing imbue the design with a recherché audacity.

Jean Paul Gaultier's signature garment is the corset-girdle. He has also played with the nineteenth-century palette and details of corsetry, as seen in his evening gown shown in the two illustrations above. Here, he corseted both the body and the arms. On the runway, the gown was worn by Sophie Dahl, a model famed for her rounded pulchritude, an exception to the prevailing angularity of fashion mannequins. Gaultier is known for his sensational and slightly scandalous runway presentations, and he certainly caused a shock as this model retreated. The back of the gown is comprised only of the corset's lacings. They are pulled taut until the knees and then open in loose loops to form a train of streamers.

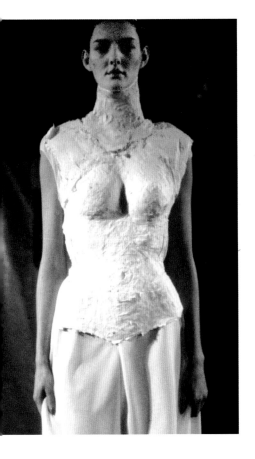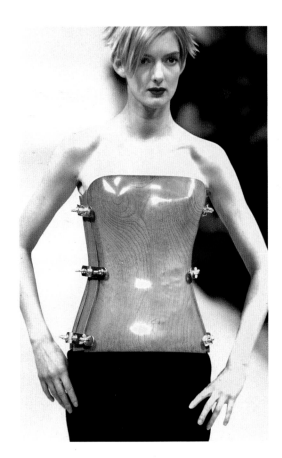

Alexander McQueen, Ensemble with molded top, "Banshee" collection, fall-winter 1994. Photograph: Chris Moore

Thierry Mugler, *Robot couture* silver cyborg suit, fall-winter 1995. Photograph: Patrice Stable

Hussein Chalayan, Wooden bustier, fall-winter 1995. Photograph: GAP JAPAN

Facing page: Issey Miyake, Red silicon bustier, 1980. The Museum at the Fashion Institute of Technology, New York, Gift of Krizia Co. (87.12.1). Photograph: Irving Solero

When the waist is the locus of intervention, the whole torso is often implicated. Severely constricting the waist causes a displacement of flesh that can generally be observed in the hips. But depending on the configuration of the corset, it may also affect the shaping of the ribcage, bust, and back. The gowns worn over corsets that imposed the wasp-waisted shapes in vogue from the 1860s to the 1890s were constructed to accommodate additional fullness. Noticeable crescents of flesh extruded from the corset's pressure at the pectoral attachment near the front arm and shoulder joint and at the back underarm.

A number of contemporary designers have addressed the whole trunk of the body with designs that appear to be a combination of armor and corsetry. Alexander McQueen blended political, social, and aesthetic narratives in work intended to provoke discussion, if not controversy. In his molded top shown above left, he took the imagery of a body cast, with its implied address of violence or injury, and he transformed the feather-plastered torso into a breastplate worthy of a Nike or Fury. Feminine vulnerability is transfigured into feminine power.

Thierry Mugler's heroines are deliberate cartoon-strip exaggerations. Like the superhumans described in the comics, Mugler's women retain an explicit sexual appeal, even as they achieve Amazonian power. In his science-fiction projection into the future, illustrated above center, the designer created an image of a woman poised in mid-transformation from flesh to metal. While armor encases much of her form, her face, breasts, and waist are exposed. The apertures are not points of vulnerability; they are opportunities for the projection of sexual attraction as a weapon.

Hussein Chalayan has played with the notion of clothing as both repressive and expressive. His bustier seen above right, with its eighteenth-century corset-like rigidity and body suppression, has the polished beauty of a coffin. In his bustier shown on the facing page, Issey Miyake took the idea of a classical breastplate and interpreted it for the Space Age. Like Mugler's, Miyake's imagery is of an idealized world of stylish superheroes.

Philippe et Gaston, Chemise, advertisement
for Philippe et Gaston couture house, 1927,
published in *Art Gout Beauté,* "Noel" issue,
1927. Photograph: Scaioni, Paris

Artist unknown, Japanese School,
Toilette (Wrapping obi), 1860s-90s. The
Metropolitan Museum of Art, Photographs,
Gift of H. de Rassloff, 1918 (1994.129).
Photograph: Mark Morosse, The Photograph
Studio, The Metropolitan Museum of Art

Facing page: Helmut Lang, Dress, fall-winter
1996. Photograph: Firstview.com

For most of the history of Western fashion, the midriff has been a major focus of design
intervention. Over time, the placement of the waist has shifted down and up, with coincident
transformations occurring in the immediately adjacent areas of the body. Invariably, the midriff
was subject to some form of constriction. In the West, the narrow waist has been a point of
beauty wherever it has been positioned.

In the 1920s, a silhouette at variance to any other period emerged. As illustrated above
left, the chemise dress, nearly planar in construction, suggested that the body was flat in front,
flat in back, and with no discernible articulation of chest, waist, or hips. Unlike the chemise
gowns of the Directoire and Empire periods or the Directoire revival of the 1910s, the 1920s
chemise admitted to no contours for the stylish body.

The articulated waist is not a universal standard. In China and many parts of Southeast
Asia and the Pacific, the waists of traditional dress are either not acknowledged by the outer
garments or are filled in with long sashes. As illustrated above right, the most familiar example
of waistline obfuscation occurs in Japan. First the kimono's wrap closure is secured by a sash.
Another sash is then twisted around the body, building up the waist to the level of the bust and
hips. An elaborate *obi,* or ornamental sash, is then wrapped around the body several times.
It terminates in a large bow-knot at the back. In some instances, the undersash has a channel
for a board. The board is similar to a corset's busk and is not intended as a bust or stomach
suppressant. Its primary function is to keep the upper body in a straight line. The ability to bend
at the natural waist is precluded, preventing the silk brocade *obi* from creasing or collapsing.

Unlike most Western interpretations of the *obi,* Helmut Lang's version, shown on the
facing page, thickens the waist as it does in the kimono. In addition, Lang's sash is so wide that
it constricts the bust. With its big bow at the back, this design cites the form of dress associated
with the decorative femininity of the Japanese geisha. But in keeping with the aesthetics of
Japanese culture—the padded waist and deemphasized bust—Lang obscured the feminine signs
of Western beauty. By transposing the body-modifying aspects of an "exotic" style as well as
the decorative effects associated with it, Lang has confronted and embraced an alternative
canon of beauty.

When the waist is obscured in fashion, the bust and hips are often camouflaged as well. In his dress shown on the facing page, Hussein Chalayan sculpted tulle into a pink pestle-shaped topiary. Because of the chin-high neckline and sloped in-fill between jawline and shoulder, the head appears to float far above the body. Because the shape of the dress splays outward from a point above the breasts, there is no evidence of the torso's contours. Except for the head and extremities, the body has been reduced to a sculptural cipher. Chalayan has examined the potent erotic and censorious possibilities of nudity and dress, often alluding to forms of conservative and traditional Muslim attire. Using the conventional materials (pink tulle) and techniques (ruffles) of a little girl's party frock, the designer muted the potential sexual impact of the female body by blending its contours into an undefined and asexual form.

Of all the designers of the mid-twentieth century, Cristobal Balenciaga was preeminent at achieving architectural effects with a minimum of technical or structural elaboration. Balenciaga's designs were so cleverly constructed that they weighed nothing. Frequently, an organza lining and air were all that supported the bold shapes he prized. Many of his designs were so voluminous that they obscured the body's actual outlines. Illustrated above left is Balenciaga's cabbage-rose cape. It is constructed of a long panel of silk gazar sewn into a bias tube. The material gathers around the torso, masking all but the head. Intermittent tacking-stitches form its petal-like folds. As shown above right, Olivier Theyskens recently took an *obi* and looped it to obliterate not only the waist but the whole of the torso. The result is an homage to Balenciaga.

Facing page: Hussein Chalayan, Dress, spring-summer 2000. Photograph: Firstview.com

Cristobal Balenciaga, *Le Chou Noir* evening cape, fall-winter 1967. Photograph: Hiro Studio

Olivier Theyskens, Cape ensemble, fall-winter 1999. Photograph: Firstview.com

In Western fashion, there are very few periods without an articulation of the waist, whether real or imagined. In the mid-1950s, Cristobal Balenciaga introduced his "Baby Doll" or tent silhouette. Unlike his "Sack Dress," which was a modified chemise, the baby doll was shaped like a cone. It was named after the type of short nightgown made notorious by the 1956 film of the same name, which starred Carroll Baker and was based on a play by Tennessee Williams. Balenciaga's original version was, however, a compromise between an expression of the waist and a denial of it. Made of lace, the tent-like gown divulged the actual contours of the body because the underdress was a fitted sheath.

By the end of his career, Balenciaga's work was characterized by increasingly rigorous technique and form. Arguably, his most masterful achievement is the wedding gown from his 1967 collection shown on the facing page. Made of two pieces of fabric stitched together for a doubled width, it has only three shaping seams: two at the shoulder and one down the back center. As the bride walked, the gown was inflated into a cone.

Equally conceptual is the ensemble by Martin Margiela illustrated above left. His layered, waist-obscuring shirt and vest are the result of taking a standard pattern and enlarging it by 148 percent. Rather than collapsing like an oversized t-shirt, the proportionally expanded garments cantilever off the body. The same frontal thrust is seen in Alexander McQueen's feathered tent, shown above right. Worn with a tight skull cap and hoof shoes by Benoit Méléard, the McQueen design suggests a chimerical pastiche: it is definitely avian, faintly reptilian, and possibly mammalian.

Facing page: Cristobal Balenciaga, Bridal gown, spring-summer 1967. Photograph: David Bailey

Martin Margiela, Oversized ensemble, fall-winter 2000. Maison Martin Margiela. Photograph: Marina Faust for Martin Margiela

Alexander McQueen, Feather dress, "Voss" collection, spring-summer 2001. Photograph: Firstview.com

92   Artist unknown, *Sir Philip Sydney*, oil on
panel, ca. 1576. Photograph: By Courtesy
of the National Portrait Gallery, London

Armor of George Clifford, third earl of
Cumberland, made in the royal workshop at
Greenwich, ca. 1580. The Metropolitan
Museum of Art, Arms and Armor, Munsey
Fund, 1932 (32.130.6)

Facing page: Issey Miyake, Pleated dress,
"Mutant Pleats" collection, fall-winter 1989.
Photograph: GAP JAPAN

The peascod jacket was affected in male dress during the last half of the sixteenth century. As evidenced in the painting reproduced above left, it is similar to the monobosom style in women's clothing that was in vogue in the first decade of the twentieth century. With both fashions, the torso was articulated as a convex form ending with a dipping waist with a sac-like overhang. In the peascod, the waist pouch was stuffed with horsehair or in some instances with straw. As exemplified in the armor shown above right, the peascod silhouette appeared simultaneously in armor of the period. Because of this, some costume scholars believe that the shaping originated as a defense against a sword's parry. Specialists in the field of arms and armor, however, believe that the opposite is true. They attribute the style to nothing other than an aesthetic development in fashionable non-martial attire that percolated into armorers' designs. In fact, innovations often occur in materials that are easily worked, as stylistic evolution can be more readily realized in those instances. But if this is the case and the peascod originated in stuffed cloth, it is nevertheless in metal that the more dramatic profiles of the fashion were finally rendered.

Although the peascod in its most explicit form was restricted to menswear, the pointed waist with rounded belly was adumbrated in some women's fashions of the day. As seen on page 144, high-style dress for sixteenth-century Venetian women, with its pointed waist rounding outward at the stomach and curving inward at the pelvis, suggested a similar interest in a protuberant abdomen.

As exemplified on the facing page, Issey Miyake introduced a peascod silhouette in 1989. He took the textile pleating techniques that have become his signature and explored their application to dress in a number of innovative directions. In this instance, he exploited the ability of pleated material to support itself in directions aligned to the folds. Miyake's design is unrelated to anything else in fashion at the time. It suggests the garb of science-fiction space warriors or pupae shedding their cocoons or larval skin. The faceted surface and the extended planes that break the body's outlines create expressionistic forms directly related to African sculptures and perhaps less directly, to the fractured effects of Analytical Cubism. Like the distended navel-out belly seen in Ivory Coast sculpture, Miyake's creation thrusts forward with a bobbing peascod profile. While his deliberate augmentation of the waistline in itself disavows the current fashion for a toned midriff, Miyake situates his work even further from the contemporary ideal of beauty by obtruding the abdomen so dramatically.

As the artificial mechanisms for creating the fashionable form have become obsolete, greater emphasis has fallen on the transformation of the body through exercise, diet, or surgical intervention. The "six-pack," the visible and defined grid of abdominal muscles, is among the most difficult aspects of the body to sustain as the body ages. Even without the incised articulation, a taut waist is almost as elusive. The low percentage of body fat and high degree of muscular development required for a rippling midriff are almost always restricted to the young, the ectomorphic, or the gym-goer.

As seen on the facing page, Alexander McQueen superimposed a muscled corselet over a classic pullover and pleated skirt ensemble to create a surrealistic X-ray effect that simulates a view of the muscles underneath the clothing. The loose sweater, often the refuge of those seeking to cocoon their form, is pulled in dramatically. But the corselet is still a camouflage. Its sculpted abdominal musculature conveys the sense of a taut and ideal form beneath, whatever the midriff's real condition and tone.

Unlike McQueen's Amazon, Issey Miyake upholstered his woman in protective padding. As seen above left, it is not only her waist that is obscured; her whole torso is stuffed to a football player's substantial bulk. By scaling up the torso, Miyake diminished the hips, and the result is a masculinized androgyny. As illustrated above right, Miyake's man's shirt alludes not to football pads but to the protective gear of the baseball catcher. The inflated horizontal bars of padding are a typical Miyake visual pun on the pumped-up-by-exercise, ripped and rippled abdominals of the male athlete.

Facing page: Givenchy Prêt-à-Porter, fall-winter 2001, Corselet ensemble, designed by Alexander McQueen. Photograph: Bruno Pellerin

Issey Miyake, Woman's shirt, fall-winter 2000. Photograph: Firstview.com

Issey Miyake, Man's shirt, spring-summer 2001. Photograph: Firstview.com

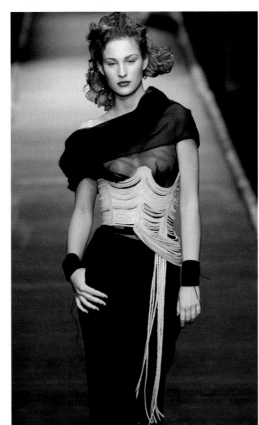

The waist as a zone of decorative focus is not exclusive to women. The Dinka people of the Sudan are virtually naked, save for their jewelry—necklaces, armlets, bracelets, anklets, and belts—and their beaded vests and corsets. Their corsets are of varying scale. As shown on the facing page, the most heroic extends from the spine to a point above the shoulders. Each is an explicit indication of age and status.

In his 1997 collection for Christian Dior, John Galliano placed interpretations of Dinka corsets and Maasai jewelry over evening gowns redolent of John Singer Sargent's famous painting of Madame X. Some of Galliano's citations are quite literal, as exemplified in the gown shown above left. In other instances, Galliano exchanged the colored seed-beads typical of the Dinka for faceted jet. The designer is well known for his post-modern strategy of anachronistic juxtaposition, and here the pairing of forms was cultural as well as historical. He assimilated his African corset into the styles of the Belle Epoque. By shifting its structure to cover the abdomen, he even mimicked the form of the *cuirasse* corset style of that period.

Looking to the same or similar ethnographic traditions, Jean Paul Gaultier cited the structure rather than the forms of the originals. In addition, his corselet shown above right is similar to the "Girdle of Venus" worn in the 1860s. Richly colored and decorated with pinked ruffles, those essentially decorative corselets were worn over the bodice and were less heavily boned than the functional corset. Bones at the front center, at the sides, and at the spine were all that were required to keep their shape and position on the body. That Gaultier's corset is equally decorative is evidenced in the loose drape of the leather lacings that connect the bones.

Facing page: Sudan, Africa, Dinka warrior, 97
late 20th century. Photograph: Angela Fisher

Christian Dior Haute Couture, spring-
summer 1997, *Kusudi* evening gown,
designed by John Galliano. Photograph:
The Fashion Group International Archives

Jean Paul Gaultier Haute Couture, Corset
ensemble, "Des robes qui se Dérobent"
collection, spring-summer 2001.
Photograph: Firstview.com

In the mid-1980s, a historicist fashion trend, inspired by the neo-Belle Epoque fantasies of Christian Lacroix, revived interest in corsets. The Lacroix couture corsets coincided with the underwear as outerwear phenomenon associated with Jean Paul Gaultier and with the post-punk street style of Vivienne Westwood. However, they had more to do with nineteenth-century forms than with either the "New Look" merry widows and girdles promoted by Gaultier or Westwood's influential bondage and eighteenth-century styles.

The preeminent contemporary corsetiere known professionally as Mr. Pearl was, and continues to be, responsible for many of the corsets presented in the French haute couture and prêt-à-porter collections including those of Lacroix. The photograph on the facing page shows Pearl himself. So corseted, he has achieved a nineteen-inch waist. Realized through traditional nineteenth-century techniques, his wasp waist introduces an S-shape effect in which the upper torso appears to be pushed forward and the abdomen shifted back. The corset's extreme constriction of the waist pulls in the flesh of the lower back and the stomach, exaggerating both the chest's forward thrust and the burgeoning of the buttocks.

The Naga of Southeast Asia and the people of Papua New Guinea practice male waist-binding. As exemplified above left, Naga men wrap themselves with long strips of cloth. In the case of the men of New Guinea, exemplified above right, the cinches are wide bands of bark incised with shallow relief patterns and painted. In both instances, the exposed body makes it obvious that in addition to emphasizing the chest and buttocks, the cinched waist serves as a foil to the pelvis. The pinched midriff throws the hipbone and groin into faintly surreal prominence. This pelvic emphasis is further accentuated by the New Guinea man, who has covered his groin with a streamer-decorated pouch suspended from a narrow corded overbelt.

Facing page: Mr. Pearl, *Corset Portrait,* 1994. Photograph: Josef Astor

Young Naga man from Southeast Asia, detail, 1913-23. Photograph: Pitt Rivers Museum, University of Oxford (B18.28e)

Man from Papua New Guinea wearing ceremonial bark belt, early 20th century. Photograph: Re/Search Publications, San Francisco

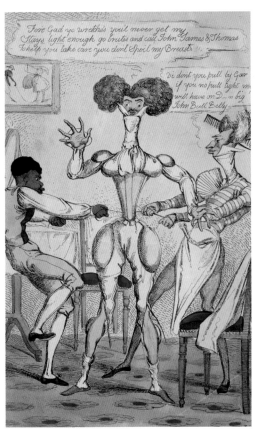

The mechanisms employed by men to achieve the effect of a slender waist were not too different from those subscribed to by their women contemporaries. The caricature of a portly gentleman being "laced" reproduced above left closely relates to Rowlandson's etching reproduced on page 78, which shows a robust lady undergoing a similarly strenuous dressing process. This man's corset, with shoulder straps and splayed hip tabs, is very like the woman's. Both corsets are intended to reshape the whole torso into a tapered cone, rather than simply cinching the waist.

Distinctions were definitely made between the desirable characteristics associated with one or the other gender. Yet it is also evident that similar attributes were applied to women and men, even if in somewhat muted form. For the eighteenth-century fashionable man and woman, a narrow back, a straightened shoulder, a longer tapering torso (at least until the 1770s), and a deeper chest were equally *à la mode.*

By the early nineteenth century, the structure of the corset was substantially lightened. The number of bones was reduced and replaced by quilted and corded channels. The net effect of this less rigid support was a lessening of impact on the shaping of the ribcage. As evidenced in the caricature shown above center, however, these more supple garments still effectively trimmed the waist and displaced the flesh—in the case of the hapless dandy—to under the arms.

Not all small waists were the consequence of corseting. The rare early nineteenth-century example of a man's drawers illustrated on the facing page shows a less draconian mode of waist suppression. A double-layered waist yoke functions as a girdle with adjustable laced tabs.

Although women's corsetry often implicated the whole torso and the upper hipline, it appears that corsets intended for men commonly addressed only the waist. The advertisement of a manufacturer of corsets for both sexes reproduced above right reiterates that a greater commitment was required of women to achieve an overall fashionable silhouette. The ideal S-curve stance, however, appears to obtain as much for men as it does for women.

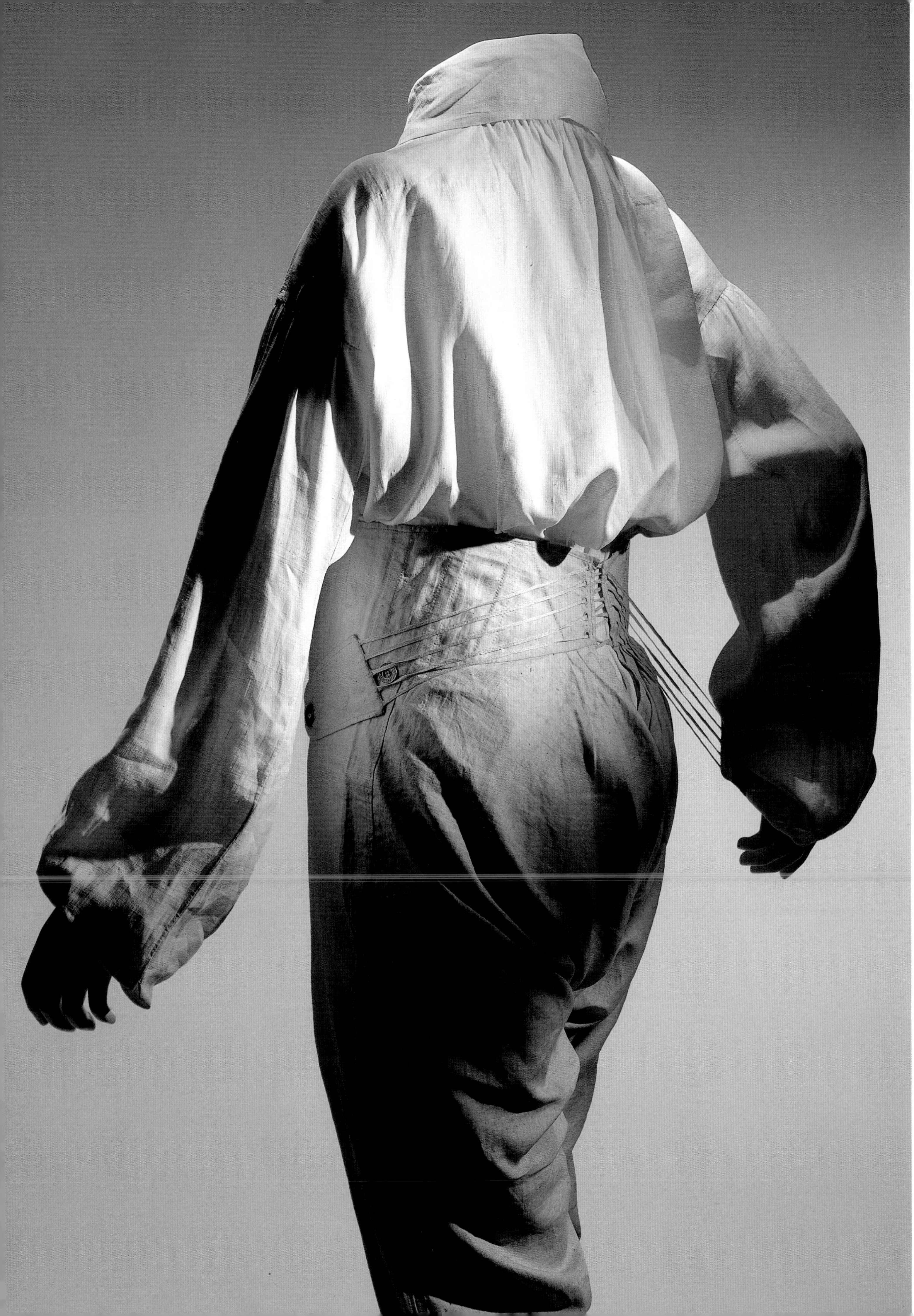

HIPS

A la mosque laide orde et sale,
est en moy la beaute principale.

...iert my met d'momaensicht al ist onreyne,
...oet dicwils spreken dat ick niet en meyn...

...inepte aume masques...pujsem...
Monstre vostre pauure orgueil hardim...

Coopt vry momaensichten en breynaet met h...
Thooft moet verciert syn, al waer themde vol kn...

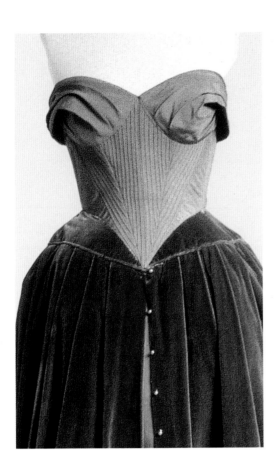

The opportunity to expand the hipline and open up the hem became a structural possibility with the introduction of the farthingale, a support worn beneath the skirt. As evidenced in *The Vanity of Women*, the engraving reproduced on the previous spread, the dilation of the hips was seen almost immediately as another expression of the idiocies of vanity and the frivolity of fashion. In his critique, the caricaturist focused on both the deformation of the body and the extravagant consumption of costly materials, which were required to conform to the new mode.

In 1947, when Christian Dior presented a collection of wasp-waisted and hip-padded designs, the American press immediately dubbed it the "New Look." The collection was a repudiation of the styles of the 1920s and 1930s, and it was also clearly indebted to the styles and body-shapers of the late nineteenth century. With the *Cigale* dress, shown on the facing page, Dior shifted the primary interest away from the waist to cantilevered hips. Unlike the emphatic hipline of previous periods portrayed in the engraving *The Vanity of Women*, Dior's creation suggested the frontal protrusion of the hipbone. The fashionable Dior posture was slightly hunched, with the back curved, the buttocks tucked under, and the pelvis pushed forward. The frontal cant of the *Cigale* skirt exaggerated the "New Look" posture.

Others in the Paris couture were also engaged in a romantic historicism. Pierre Balmain cited historical precedents in his "open robe," an eighteenth-century style characterized by a fitted bodice, overskirt, and visible underskirt. More than to any true historical precedent, Balmain's selective adaptation of period details situates the gown illustrated above left closer to the sensibility of the costumes by Jean Cocteau and Christian Bérard for the 1945 film *Beauty and the Beast*. But the dress's padded hipline also quite accurately revives the panniered and farthingaled silhouettes of earlier periods.

In her design shown above right, Alix Grès externalized hip pads like vestiges of a farthingale. Her hip crescents also allude to the small pads attached to eighteenth-century corsets. The pads extended the hipline, and they also provided a "catch" for the waistbands of silhouette-expanding panniers. Grès is renowned for her Neoclassical pleated gowns. Here she used her signature pleating to introduce more volume to the skirt in addition to the hipline. Uncharacteristically, Grès deviated in this design from her principle of columnar elegance and resorted to a surprising body modification.

Overleaf: After Maarten de Vos, *The Vanity of Women: Masks and Bustles*, engraving, ca. 1600. The Metropolitan Museum of Art, The Costume Institute, Purchase, Irene Lewisohn Trust, 2001 (2001.341.1). Photograph: Mark Morosse, The Photograph Studio, The Metropolitan Museum of Art

Facing page: Christian Dior, *Cigale* dinner dress, fall-winter 1952. Photograph: Frances MacLaughlin-Gill, courtesy of Peter Fetterman Gallery, Santa Monica, California

Pierre Balmain, Evening gown, ca. 1951. The Museum at the Fashion Institute of Technology, New York, Gift of Mrs. F. Leval (84.125.3). Photograph: Irving Solero

Alix Grès, Day dress, 1949-52. The Museum at the Fashion Institute of Technology, New York, Gift of Mrs. Molly Milbank (91.253.2). Photograph: Irving Solero

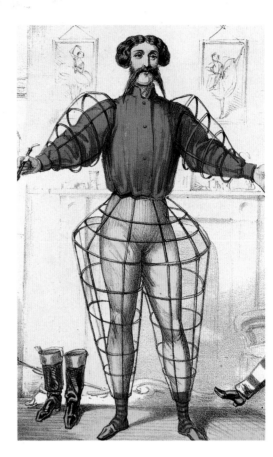

Monogrammist LAM, *Portrait of a Man in White,* oil on wood, 16th century. The Metropolitan Museum of Art, European Paintings, The Friedsam Collection, Bequest of Michael Friedsam, 1931 (32.100.119)

Anonymous German Artist, *Cavalier,* engraving, ca. 1580. The Metropolitan Museum of Art, Drawings and Prints, Harris Brisbane Dick Fund, 1953 (53.601.337). Photograph: Mark Morosse, The Photograph Studio, The Metropolitan Museum of Art

Anonymous, British, *The Progress,* detail, hand-colored lithograph, ca. 1830. The Metropolitan Museum of Art, Drawings and Prints, Elisha Whittelsey Collection, The Elisha Whittelsey Fund, 1971 (1971.564.26). Photograph: Mark Morosse, The Photograph Studio, The Metropolitan Museum of Art

Facing page: Thierry Mugler, *Apron* dress, spring-summer 1991. Photograph: Patrice Stable

The farthingale and later the pannier, or side hoop, supported extensions of the skirt and served to further diminish by contrast the already corset-cinched girth of the waist. The exaggerations of women's dress were often reflected in modified form in male garb. The rounded trunk hose worn by the figure in *Portrait of a Man in White,* the painting reproduced above left, typified Western men's dress from the late fifteenth to the early seventeenth century. The ballooning of fabric from the narrow pointed waist is similar in construction to skirts of the day.

The balloon-hipped silhouette of the trunk hose could also be seen in longer trousers of the period. As illustrated in the engraving reproduced above center, they were rounded over the hip and upper thigh and then tapered to the knee. The rounded hip was concurrent with a modified gigot sleeve. A similar silhouette was revived in the 1820s and 1830s. At that time, the inflation was seen as so dramatically different from the previous period's skin-tight fit that the caricaturist who made the illustration shown above right proposed an infrastructure to sustain its forms. Such elaborate structures never developed, but the humorist's cage presaged the invention of the crinoline hoop for women by more than a decade.

Trunk hose, with their layers, interfacings, and linings, were highly upholstered. Thierry Mugler referenced that quality of padded volume in a dress of 1991, shown on the facing page. It is cropped to a height similar to that of a Renaissance man's trunk hose. Mugler merged elements from panniers and trunk hose with the look of a 1950s American housewife's gingham apron. He thus conflated history, gender, and class in his whimsical pastiche.

Small pads were attached below the waistline of eighteenth-century corsets like the ones illustrated above. The hip pads took the shape of bolster-like rolls, crescents, or rectangular pads. These were designed to support the skirt directly, as well as the structures like panniers, or side hoops, over which the increasingly large skirts of the period were draped. As evidenced by the exquisite brocaded silk-taffeta English court dress shown on the following spread, a panniered skirt might reach six to eight feet in width.

As illustrated on the facing page, Rei Kawakubo has played with the notion of the hip pad. She distended, shifted, and even cloned its eccentric form across the hips and over the torso and shoulders. Her designs from this collection were used by the choreographer Merce Cunningham for a dance piece titled *Scenario*. For Cunningham, the designs recalled "a man in a raincoat and a backpack" and "a woman in shorts with a baby on her side ... shapes we see everyday." In Cunningham's work, the dancers spiral across the stage like tops. The somewhat unnerving "bumps" that would appear to inhibit the body's movement instead introduce an upholstered security to the dancer's propulsive turns.

Kawakubo questions the notion of symmetry as an essential component of healthful and attractive physiques. For her, beauty appears to reside even in an asymmetry that evokes the presence of medical pathologies. Kawakubo's design underscores the fact that the uneasiness precipitated by her aesthetic does not simply derive from its distortion of the natural form but rather from the asymmetry she introduces. But even in its deformity, her faintly monstrous restructuring of the natural body is nowhere near the exaggerated scale of the panniered gowns that were in vogue in the eighteenth century.

Facing page: Comme des Garçons, "The dress meets the body. The body meets the dress. And they are one." collection, spring-summer 1997, *Bump* dress, designed by Rei Kawakubo. Photograph: Paolo Roversi for Japanese *Marie-Claire*

European, Two corsets with hip pads, third quarter 18th century. The Metropolitan Museum of Art, The Costume Institute, Gifts of Mrs. Lee Simonson, 1939 (CI39.13.211; CI39.13.206a,b). Photograph: Karin L. Willis, The Photograph Studio, The Metropolitan Museum of Art

Overleaf: English, *Robe à la française*, ca. 1750. The Metropolitan Museum of Art, The Costume Institute, Purchase, Irene Lewisohn Bequest, 1965 (CI 65.13.1a-c). Photograph: Karin L. Willis, The Photograph Studio, The Metropolitan Museum of Art

In the eighteenth century, formal dress was so closely associated with Versailles and the French court that it was universally described as the *robe à la française*. As illustrated above left, the *robe à la française* has a fitted overdress. It is open at the front, with a decorative bodice insert called a stomacher covering the corset and an underskirt, the petticoat, showing under the splayed drapery of the overskirt.

In its most formal configuration, the *robe à la française* presented a particularly wide and flattened profile accomplished by enlarged panniers. Constructed of supple bent wands of willow or whalebone and covered in linen, panniers took on broader or narrower silhouettes. The most remarkable, like the one on the previous spread, held out the skirt like sandwich boards, barely wider than the body in side view but as expansive as possible in front or rear view. As shown in the etching *Les Adieux*, reproduced above right, a woman so garbed had to pass through a doorway sideways.

John Webber's engraving, reproduced on the facing page, portrays a young woman of Otaheite (Tahiti). Her costume bears a marked resemblance to eighteenth-century European court dress. It is difficult to know how much the courtly aesthetic of the *robe à la française* influenced the documentary impulse of this British artist as he traveled and sketched throughout the South Pacific. In that part of the world, the use of the large field of barkcloth as a backdrop for the two feather fans—borne on the skirt and intended as gifts—is an explicit manifestation of prestige. Through an extravagant use of rare materials and a surprisingly similar strategy for display, the most formal panniered gowns in the West were equally, if less obviously, an opportunity for expressing wealth and rank. As in eighteenth-century Tahiti, contemporary fashionable European aristocrats in gowns like those shown above exploited the broad front of their skirts for the liberal application of silver and gold lace or silk fly-fringe embellished robings as a sign of their social and economic privilege.

Facing page: Bartolozzi after John Webber, *A Young Woman of Otaheite, bringing a present*, engraving, 1784, from Cook and King, *A Voyage to the Pacific Ocean*. Photograph: Mark Morosse, The Photograph Studio, The Metropolitan Museum of Art

French or Austrian, *Robe à la française*, ca. 1765. The Metropolitan Museum of Art, The Costume Institute, Purchase, Irene Lewisohn Bequest, 2001. Photograph: Karin L. Willis, The Photograph Studio, The Metropolitan Museum of Art

Robery Delaunay after Jean-Michel Moreau le jeune, *Les Adieux*, etching, published in *Monument of Costume*, 1777. The Metropolitan Museum of Art, Drawings and Prints, Purchase, 1934 (34.22.1). Photograph: Mark Morosse, The Photograph Studio, The Metropolitan Museum of Art

The pannier that structured the wide-hipped outline of the formal eighteenth-century gown has inspired a number of revivals, if in only modified form. Its most surprising occurrence was in the 1920s, when the reigning silhouette was the straight up and down, flat in front and back, chemise associated with the flapper and the jazz age. However, coincident with the androgynous, board-like effect of the chemise was an alternative, the *robe de style*. This latter form of dress, also without bust, waist, or buttocks in evidence, nevertheless conveyed the femininity of the wearer through rich surface ornament. Although it resembles the chemise in the bodice, the *robe de style* has a wide, pannier-supported, ankle-length skirt. Jeanne Lanvin, famed for her romantic, often historicist designs, was a major proponent of the style, as were the Boué Soeurs.

The Boués began as specialists in lingerie, but soon were successfully creating almost excessively feminine party frocks embellished with their signature silk ribbon rosettes, often as *robes de styles* like the one illustrated on the facing page. Because of the delicate handkerchief-weight fabrics they employed, the wire panniers that supported the hips of a Boué Soeur gown could often be seen. The contrast of the engineered hoops with the ethereal hand-embroidered linen, lace, and silk ribbons suggests the theatrical artifice of the Boué style.

Designers' recent historical citations of eighteenth-century side hoops are more ironic. The anachronisms of Jean Paul Gaultier's "The Charms of Frida Kahlo" collection are combined in the ensemble shown above left. Here, Gaultier merged aspects of riding habits and the tuxedo jacket with the silhouette of the eighteenth-century *amazone*. With its black taffeta stock coming undone, this ensemble equally evokes the huntress returning disheveled from her ride and the somber attire of a woman in perpetual mourning. The allusion to riding invests the breadth of the panniers with a humorous saddlebag effect. On the other hand, Yohji Yamamoto's deconstructivist design of 1995 illustrated above right cites eighteenth-century panniers. Those hip extenders were named for straw baskets, but in Yamamoto's design, where they are silhouetted against a crimson lining, they are more like iron cages, reminiscent of the grills used by iron workers to heat coals and suggestive of devices worthy of the Spanish Inquisition.

Facing page: Boué Soeurs, *Robe de style* with panniers, ca. 1923. Courtesy of Mark Walsh. Photograph: Karin L. Willis, The Photograph Studio, The Metropolitan Museum of Art

Jean Paul Gaultier, Ensemble, "The Charms of Frida Kahlo" collection, spring-summer, 1998. Photograph: Firstview.com

Yohji Yamamoto, Crinoline dress, fall-winter 1995. Photograph: GAP JAPAN

English, Petticoat bustle, ca. 1871. The
Metropolitan Museum of Art, The Costume
Institute, Purchase, New-York Historical
Society (by exchange) and Louise Moore
Van Vleck Gift, 1985 (1985.27.4).
Photograph: Karin L. Willis, The Photograph
Studio, The Metropolitan Museum of Art

Oskar Schlemmer, *Spiral Figurine, Black
Series,* "Screw" costume from *The Triadic
Ballet,* 1922, reconstructed 1991.
Photograph: Photo Archive C. Raman
Schlemmer

Junya Watanabe, Ensemble, fall-winter
1998. Photograph: Firstview.com

Facing page: *Couturière élégante allant
livrer son ouvrage,* etching, 1778-87,
published in Emile Levy, ed., *Galerie des
Modes et Costumes Français Dessinés
d'Après Nature,* Paris, Librairie Centrale
des Beaux-Arts. Photograph: Mark Morosse,
The Photograph Studio, The Metropolitan
Museum of Art

By the mid-nineteenth century, industrial processes had merged with the fashion system and supported an unprecedented acceleration of style changes. Publishing, textile production, sewing, and transport contributed decisively to the dissemination of new fashions. The technical engineered solutions to problems embraced at that time extended to the development of engineered corsets, crinoline hoops, and bustles like the one shown above left.

The idea of this fan-like rather than tent-like extension is the structural basis of the 1922 costume design by Oskar Schlemmer shown above center. In this "Screw" costume for his *Triadic Ballet,* a metal blade rotates around the body from waist to hem.

In the eighteenth-century print shown on the facing page, a woman who sells panniers is transporting her wares. The image provides a rare contemporary view of a pannier off the body. Collapsed, it becomes a flat oval rather than the three-dimensional half-basket more typically rendered in caricatures and engravings of the time. This taut plane of stretched fabric is among the precedents for Junya Watanabe's 1998 skirt, shown above right. The design also references the engineered constructions of late-nineteenth-century bustles and the abstractions of early-twentieth-century Constructivism. Watanabe mined these varied sources, and with the flat disk that circles the waist, he introduced the additional reference of the couturier's spiraling draping process. In Watanabe's rendering, the dress becomes a chemise-like form on which a mutated pannier revolves and devolves.

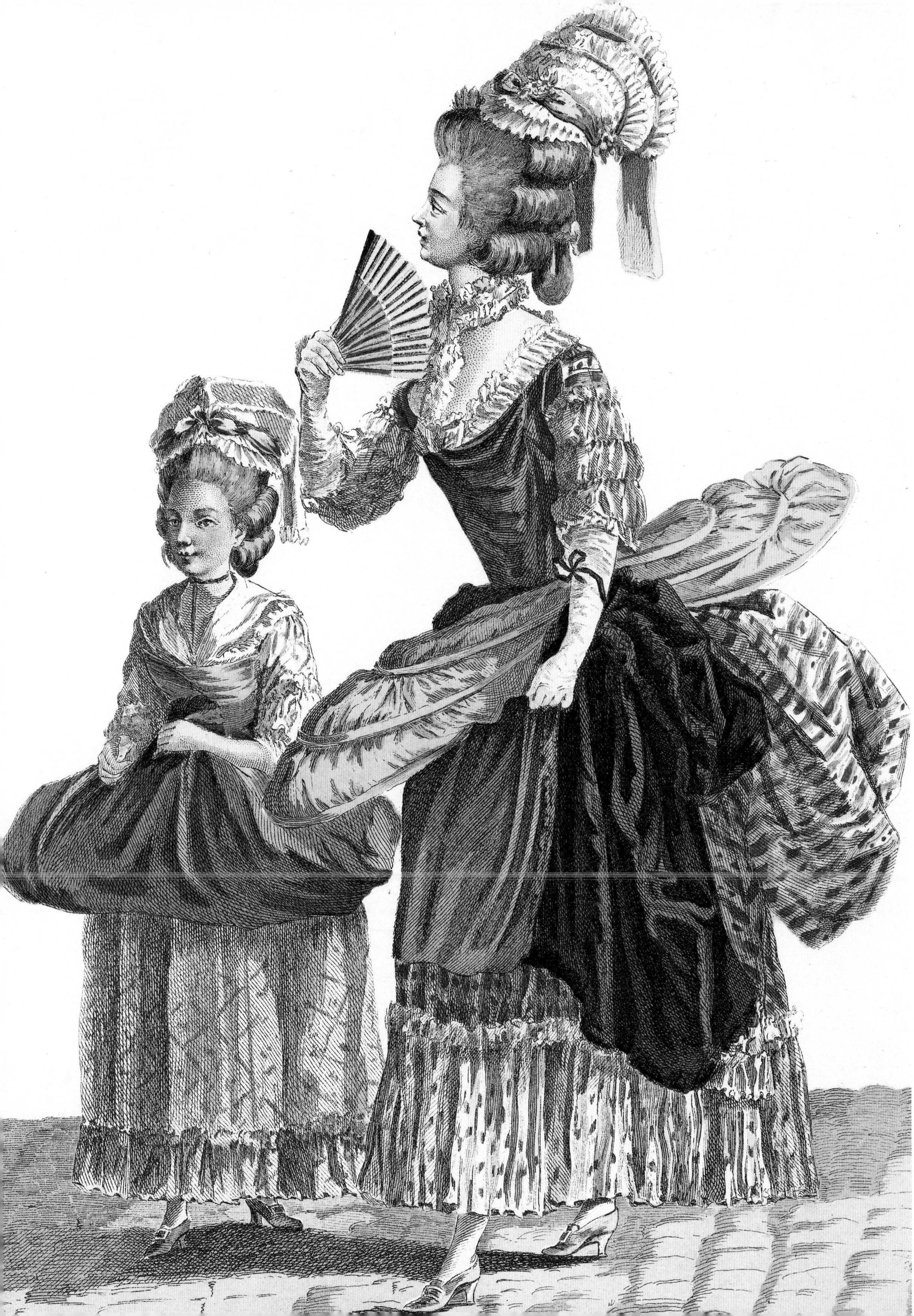

The ideal of a burgeoning skirt is not restricted to the West. In the Pacific Islands, tapa (bark cloth), palm fronds, and shredded *ti*-leaves are used. In Africa, grass is built up into huge mounded forms. The two adolescents of the Northern Congo Ngbende people depicted on the facing page are dressed for their initiation into womanhood. Their faces are fringed with grass to hide their juvenile identities until the end of the ceremony, when they are revealed in a transformed state of womanhood. In the context of the ritual, their skirts can be seen as a metaphor for the expansion of the unarticulated contours of the girl to the widened pelvis of the newly nubile woman.

With her highly informed and invariably provocative aesthetic, Rei Kawakubo has advanced historical forms of dress using radical functional and structural transpositions. Kawakubo introduced the historicist romanticism of Christian Dior, Jacques Fath, and Charles James to her "Sweeter than Sweet" collection. Vague references to the eighteenth and nineteenth centuries are also suggested. This kind of Postmodernist conflation resulted in the almost Dadaist effect of her pannier dress, illustrated above left. The skirt is shaped like a coat, with its sleeves flattened, its neckline at the waist, and its back to the front. The jacket's compressed shoulders are supported by an explosion of tulle, the likes of which had not been seen since the crinolined extravaganzas of the 1950s.

The Versace gown shown above right has a cropped overdress and a trained underskirt. This take on the eighteenth century recalls the gold festooned costume of Louis XIV dressed as Apollo. Like the rigorous symmetricality of its eighteenth-century precedents, this 1999 design creates a structured bell shape. The designer referenced the ingnious cut of Dior's *Cigale* dress in the unusual construction of the doubled skirt's protuberant hipline. In motion, the separation of dress and underskirt causes the ensemble to sway hypnotically.

Facing page: North Congo, Africa, Ngbende initiates wearing grass skirts, late 20th century. Photograph: Carol Beckwith and Angela Fisher

Comme des Garçons, "Sweeter than Sweet" collection, fall-winter 1995, Evening gown, designed by Rei Kawakubo. Photograph: Firstview.com

Versace Haute Couture, fall-winter 1999, Evening gown, designed by Donatella Versace. Photograph: Firstview.com

From the 1830s to the 1850s, skirts achieved a fashionable bell-shaped volume through a layering of corded or ruffled petticoats, often heavily starched. In the 1850s, innovative wired hoops connected by canvas tapes eliminated the layers of underclothing and also allowed for a previously unattainable volume. Although the hips were necessarily expanded by the hoops, the real inflation was in the circumference of the skirt's hem.

By the 1860s, with the endorsement of Charles Frederick Worth, the preeminent couturier of his day, the crinoline hoop reached breathtaking proportions. As exemplified in the lithograph reproduced above, it caught the imagination not only of the fashionable *mondaine* but also of the caricaturist. Similar space-devouring volumes were not attempted again until the 1950s, with the historicist post "New Look" collections of the French couture and the wildly imaginative work of the American designer Charles James. Unlike the airy, if massive, umbrella-like skirts of the 1860s, however, the ball gowns of a Dior, Jacques Fath, or James were heavily constructed. In some of the more elaborate post-World War II designs, net, crinoline tapes, wire, and other interfacings were employed over layers of canvas to create the sculpted form of ball gowns.

Recently, Alexander McQueen attempted to return to the lighter effects of the Second Empire to inflate his silhouettes. In his design shown on the facing page, McQueen employed a spun-sugar-like shell reinforced by plastic to engineer the gown's awesome expanse.

The gown of even greater expanse shown on the following spread was created by John Galliano for Dior. As the eponymous founder of the house had done, Galliano mined the refinements of the eighteenth century. In this design, he combined the parts of a *robe à la française* with the crinolined silhouette of the mid-nineteenth-century Second Empire period. The result is a skirt nine feet wide, with a train that extends it even farther.

Facing page: Givenchy Haute Couture, spring-summer 2000, Evening gown, designed by Alexander McQueen. Photograph: Bruno Pellerin

Read's Crinoline Sketches, No. 9, hand-colored lithograph, published by Read & Co., July 22, 1859. The Metropolitan Museum of Art, Drawings and Prints, Elisha Whittelsey Collection, Elisha Whittelsey fund, 1963 (63.617.10). Photograph: Mark Morosse, The Photograph Studio, The Metropolitan Museum of Art

Overleaf: Dior Haute Couture, *Maria-Luisa (dite Corée)* gown, spring-summer 1998, designed by John Galliano. The Metropolitan Museum of Art, The Costume Institute, Gift of Christian Dior Haute Couture, Paris, 1999 (1999.494a). Photograph: Karin L. Willis, The Photograph Studio, The Metropolitan Museum of Art

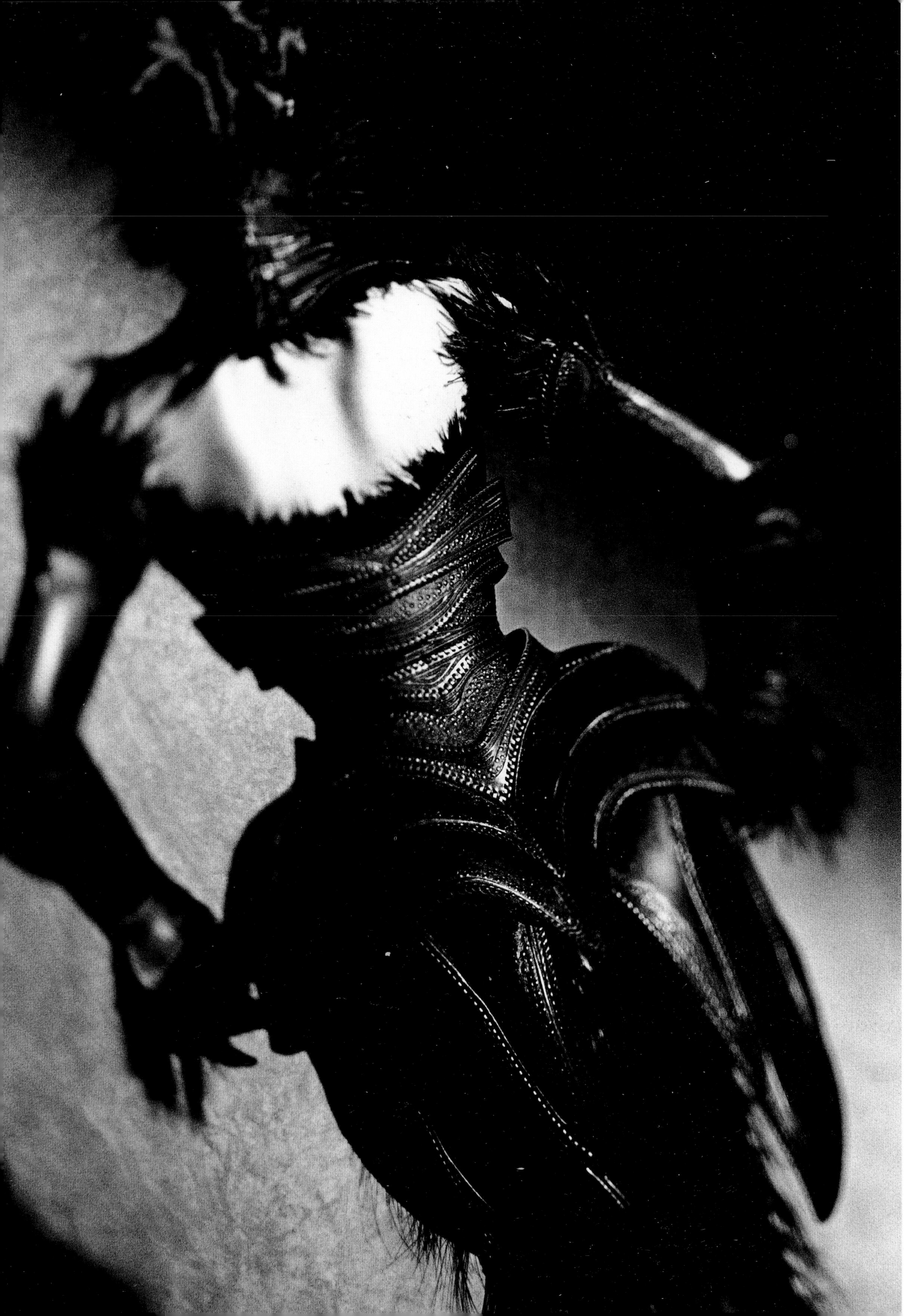

The bustled skirts of the 1870s had the surprising puffed effect and induced waddle of Cochin bantam hens. More architectonic bustles developed at a later date. As seen in the three examples shown above, the crinoline hoops that evolved from the crinolines of the 1860s took on a more cylindrical form, with a flattened front and increased emphasis over the buttocks.

Although they were conceived purely as an adjunct to the achieving of an aesthetic effect, crinoline hoops also responded to practical considerations. The one shown above right, called the lobster-pot, has a button-on hem ruffle and is constructed of medium-weight wool. Like winter petticoats of the period, it was designed to keep the wearer warm. This was in addition to at least four layers of underclothing and the heavily ornamented outer clothing typically worn at that time.

As exemplified in the dress on the facing page, the bustle was at its greatest extension by 1885. It was almost perpendicular to the back and was heavily upholstered. Earlier manifestations of the style were loosely gathered balloons of fabric not dissimilar to Austrian shades; they were volumetric and buoyant in effect. The 1880s versions were as padded and heavily embellished as a drawing-room hassock of the period. It was a popular conceit that the cantilevers of these bustles could support an entire tea service. To sustain the greater weight of the 1880s gowns, crinoline hoops were webbed across the back of the legs so that the bustle was held in place and did not swing forward. These inventive infrastructures were made of light and flexible materials—wire, cane, whalebone—held together by canvas tapes or inserted into quilted channels.

Facing page: American, Evening dress, ca. 1884-86. The Metropolitan Museum of Art, The Costume Institute, Gift of Mrs. J. Randall, 1963 (CI63.23.3a,b). Photograph: Karin L. Willis, The Photograph Studio, The Metropolitan Museum of Art

American, Crinoline hoops, The Metropolitan Museum of Art, The Costume Institute. Left: 1870s, Gift of Mrs. Robert K. Baker, 1963 (CI63.12.1). Center: 1880s, Gift of Miss Marian H. Smith, 1979 (1979.53.2). Right: Lobster-pot crinoline hoop, ca. 1885, Gift of Lee Simonson, 1938 (CI38.23.281). Photograph: Karin L. Willis, The Photograph Studio, The Metropolitan Museum of Art

Hussein Chalayan, Dress with bustle, spring-summer 2000. Photograph: Firstview.com

Viktor and Rolf, White bustle suit, "Collection 02," 1994. Photograph: Wendelien Daan

A.F. Vandervorst, Saddle coat, fall-winter 1998. Photograph: A. F. Vandervorst

Facing page: Yohji Yamamoto, Tulle bustle coat, fall-winter 1986. Photograph: Nick Knight for Yohji Yamamoto

The exaggerated bustle, with its imposition of a swinging, side-to-side gait, often suggested animal counterparts to nineteenth-century satirists, an aspect of the style that seems to resonate with designers today. Nick Knight's photograph of Yohji Yamamoto's design reproduced on the facing page emphasizes the similarity of the ensemble to the profile of an ornamental bantam rooster. Yamamoto's design reinterprets many of the details of the 1880s with irony. The swooping duck-billed bonnet of that period becomes a visored baseball cap, the ankle boots are reduced to mannish Oxfords, and the heavily draped bustle skirt and wired understructures are etherealized as a puff of synthetic organza.

Hussein Chalayan has proposed affinities in the design arts. In his spring-summer 2000 collection, Chalayan devised furniture pieces that could be transformed into apparel. As exemplified above left, the collection also included garments conceived of as containers. Chalayan articulated his molded forms like the flaps of a jet plane's cargo hold. When open, they take on a pannier-like width and bustle-form extension.

Viktor and Rolf conflate the *robe à la française*, eighteenth-century male dress, and the 1870s for period effect in their suit shown above center. In a very short time, these designers have established a reputation for conceptually driven, technically sophisticated, historically informed creations. Above all, the intellectual complexity of their work is saved from pedantry by a whimsical irony.

The Belgian design team of A.F. Vandervorst literally saddles the body in the coat shown above right. The effect is simultaneously of orthopedic brace, back-pack, *obi*, and bustle. John Galliano's more extravagantly comedic equine ensemble shown on page 103 is an Ovidian transmutation. The cantilever of two saddlebags and a tail-like fall of horsehair creates a bustle extension equal to any from the 1880s. One of Galliano's irrefutable gifts is his ability to combine the most theatrical effects with components of dress and accessories that are eminently wearable, as the ubiquitous appearance of his saddle bag on stylish clients has confirmed.

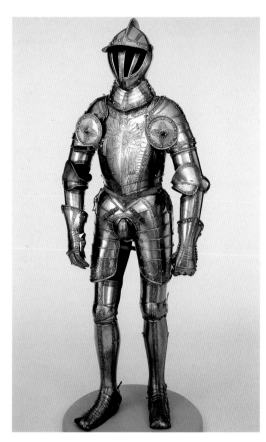

Paolo Veronese, *Boy with a Greyhound*,
oil on canvas, 1570s. The Metropolitan
Museum of Art, European Paintings,
H.O. Havemeyer Collection, Bequest of
Mrs. H.O. Havemeyer, 1929 (29.100.105).
Photograph: Peter Zeray, The Photograph
Studio, The Metropolitan Museum of Art

Attributed to Kunz Lochner, Armor of
Emperor Ferdinand I, 1549. The
Metropolitan Museum of Art, Arms and
Armor, Gift of George D. Pratt and Rogers
Fund, 1933 (33.164a-x)

Facing page: West New Guinea, Kapauku
headman, 1954-55. Photograph:
Dr. Leopold J. Pospisil

In the West, the prosthetic extension and ornamentation of the penis were elaborations of the covering—required by modesty—for the breach at the crotch that characterized early male leggings. The rapid move from early modestly and functionally shaped triangles to greater embellishment is, perhaps, a predictable aesthetic response. As exemplified in the painting by Paolo Veronese above left, the crotch piece matches the rich effects of the trunk hose, in fabric and in ornament.

The impulse to pad, extend, and re-form the crotch piece was certainly not a functional response. Thickened, snub-nosed, angled upward, or splayed at its base, the codpiece is as much an abstraction of the body part as the cone bra of the 1940s and 1950s. At its most highly evolved state, the sculpted codpiece became a purely expressive form, neither a covering for modesty nor a structural support for the genitals. The nature of variation in the redesign of the male member's cover can be seen in armorial examples like the one shown above right.

Interestingly, it is in cultures where notions of Western modesty are irrelevant that it is possible to find similar instances of refashioned phalluses. As illustrated on the facing page, the Kapauku headmen of New Guinea wear ithyphallic covers that have no protective function. They are woven in grass or cane into long tapered cylinders and are strapped to the body. While the effect is one of exaggerated distension, the tapering of the casing's tip suggests the dormant, hooded, uncircumcised organ. A morphology of repose is rendered in the scale of arousal, which may be the point. The woven covers are not the evidence of an aggressive priapism but rather of the heroic potential to achieve one.

FEET

Hans Holbein, *Henry VIII*, oil on panel, 1536. Photograph: Board of Trustees of the National Museums and Galleries on Merseyside (Walker Art Gallery, Liverpool)

Vittore Carpaccio, *Two Venetian Women*, oil on panel, ca. 1500. Museo Correr, Venice. Photograph: Copyright Alinari / Art Resource, New York

Overleaf: W&LT (Wild and Lethal Trash), Man's stilt ensemble, "A Fetish for Beauty" collection, spring-summer 1998. Photograph: Firstview.com

Shoes have been the most persistent example of fashion's imposition of an idealized form on the natural anatomy. Even in civilizations of the warmest climes, where footwear is invariably a form of flat sandal, the outline of the sole is often idealized through an abstracting symmetry. However, it is the more fully shod foot that has been the primary focus of dramatic physical manipulation. The elaboration of footwear as it pertains to the distortion of the body occurs in three primary ways: the shaping of the uppers, especially the configuration of the toe-cap; the thickening of the sole; and the elevation of the heel.

Much of the fashionable footwear of today derives from fourteenth-century European precedents. But earlier, in the Byzantine period, sock-like uppers were already depicted with either rounded or center-pointed tips. A shape more conforming to the foot's outline is represented in the Reims Cathedral, in the chainmail covered leggings of the Melchizedek figure from the mid-thirteenth century. But the pointed center-tipped shoe also appears in this period with enough regularity to suggest that it was a commonly occurring style.

The modeling of the right and left shoe in shapes that reflect the indentation at the arch of the foot dates from the late twelfth or early thirteenth century. Additional stylistic details that were more explicit indications of the individuation of the left and right shoe came in the form of mirror images in the side-lacings, latches, or straps, and later, in button closures. But despite the differentiation imposed by the structural conformity of the shoe to each foot, the forepart of the sole and the uppers were often absolutely symmetrical. Surprisingly, this can even be seen in Early Dynastic Egyptian sandals. Made of woven palm leaves, their soles extended to points that are anchored to the intersection of the arch and toe straps. The curving of the sole over the toes created a squared, prow-like form that camouflaged the foot's actual shape.

The distortion of the foot is most clearly expressed in the abstraction of the shoe's forepart. Although rounded, square, and blunt capped shoe styles are more accommodating of the foot, they generally did not reflect the actual angled arrangement of toes. While there have been periods where a blunt fronted shoe did reflect the foot's general shape, even designs that concede the natural spread of feet from heel to toes tend to exaggerate the outline. In mid-sixteenth century England, for example, the width of the shoe, measured across the sole, could approach six inches. As seen in Henry VIII's portrait reproduced at the upper left, the elaboration of the front into a hammer-head outline, called the "horned" toe, further enhanced the breadth of the foot. A century later, a narrower squared-toe extended the foot's length and ended with a flattened tip. In periods with square-toed fashions, therefore, the foot appeared in a variety of forms, including a truncated splay in the Tudor period and a "forked" duckbill shape in the mid-seventeenth century.

The most symmetrical and square-toed shoes appear in the nineteenth century. From the 1830s to the 1860s, these shoes, similar to ballet slippers, were idealized in the outline of their soles. Called straights, they had no distinction between the left or right sole, suggesting that the feet were barely articulated cylinders. In addition fashion illustrations of the day establish that the very narrow foot best manifested the prevailing standard of beauty.

The shoe that comes to a centered point is even less representative of the foot's natural form than the squared toe. Still, the pointed toe has been a recurrent theme in the history of shoe design. Its most extravagant development occurred in the late Gothic period, from the end of the fourteenth century to the late fifteenth century. Called the *poulaine, cracow*, or pike, this style had a pointed toe extending to four or more inches. Although longer examples do not survive, there are manuscript depictions of toe-points so attenuated that they required anchoring at the knee or even at the waist. However, some costume historians question the documentary veracity of such representations. In the few authentic extant examples, the toe-points were made turgid by stuffing. They curl slightly upward, which presumably precluded the continuous stubbing the wearer would endure if the tips pointed straight out.

When shoes are configured into extreme points, the toes adapt somewhat over time to the triangular shaping. In essence, the form of the shoe consistently worn eventually molds the foot. Generally, the big toe is deviated at the second joint and angled inward in the opposite direction from the first metatarsal bone, which normally fans out. The small outer toe is also subjected to pressure, which, though it coincides with the toe's natural inward curl, is at a much more emphatic angle. This deformation of the natural foot, with some attendant medical consequences, has done little to alter the repetitive cycle of pointed-toed shoe fashions.

The most apparent distortion of the foot historically is the past Chinese practice of foot-binding. Current scholarship has attempted to extrapolate from the often lurid Chinese and Western depictions of the practice a more objective view of the long history of the Golden Lotus, as the bound foot was euphemistically called. Although it is still somewhat conjectural, many specialists in Chinese studies have recently come to believe that foot-binding originated in the tenth century and had become commonplace by the thirteenth century. The Golden Lotus was the result of the deliberate reformation of the foot through systematic binding that precipitated the collapsing of the instep and the folding under of all but the big toe. This was done to conform to a cultural ideal of feet of bud-like shape and diminished size. Lotus slippers are therefore not the precipitants of any deformation, as pointed-toed stiletto-heeled shoes might reasonably be argued to be. They are merely the decorative evidence of an excruciatingly painful transformation.

While the foot has been shaped to a fashionable ideal by the artificial constraints of soles and uppers, it has also been subject to adjustment in another way. By the addition of layers of leather or risers of cork, wood, or any material of a relatively light weight, the sole can be thickened and the shoe elevated. The shapes of risers have varied from flat boards, to cylindrical posts, to thickened wedges. The sole has been lifted anywhere from less than an inch to over twenty inches, as seen in the sixteenth-century Venetian *chopines* shown in the illustration at the lower left. Historically, this mode of raising the wearer off the ground has not been rationalized, either for the aesthetic advantage gained in height or for the functional remove they provided from muddy unpaved streets. Instead, the platform sole's impairment of a woman's walk was seen as a way to control her morality, since mobility was directly associated in many cultures and times with the potential for unrestrained sexuality.

Of course, the obverse was also true. Both the courtesans of Venice on their *chopines* and the *Oiran* of the *Yoshiwara*, the quarter of the "Floating World," wearing their *dochu-geta*, were known for their slow progress when walking through the streets. These shoe styles lifted women higher than the norm, endowing them with a greater public stature. Their encumbered walking was also an asset; it imposed a slow ceremonial gait that allowed the crowds to study the courtesan's beauty and fashions more closely.

More than the thickening and lifting of the sole, it is the introduction of the heel that has had the most dramatic impact on the shoe's relationship to the body. The high heel redirects the wearer's balance and engages the front pad and toes in sustaining much of the body's weight. Not surprisingly, X rays of the foot in a stiletto heel and of the bound lotus foot disclose a redistribution of weight similar to that experienced by ballet dancers *en pointe*. The tip-toe effect might account for the appeal of a high heel shoe's profile. The foot angled upward by a heel is imbued with an antigravitational elevation and visual insubstantiality shared by the Golden Lotus and the toe shoes worn by Degas's ballet dancers illustrated at the upper right.

The heel and the arched sole that is its consequence began with the wedged angled sole, lower in front than at the heel and with the shaped platform of the *chopine*, both of which had their origins in the mid-sixteenth century. The late 1500s witnessed the introduction of shoes with high heels and a curved arch, but the style only became commonplace in the seventeenth century, when shoes reached as much as two-to-three inches at their highest. Although the high heel had initially been rounded, this was soon modified with its front face clearly squared. By the mid-seventeenth century, the profile of this heel took on a waisted, or pinched, outline that was to predominate thereafter. The arched sole with elevated heel persisted through most of the eighteenth century but was replaced by a lower slipper-like style toward the end of the century. The high heel was not to return into vogue until the 1860s. At that date, the heel was generally of modest dimension, but by the end of the decade, they could be over two inches high. As the century came to a close, fashionable shoes were known to have heels approaching four or more inches. However, with the quick extinction of the very high heel as fashionable footwear, the two-inch and two-and-a-half-inch heel became the norm in the early twentieth century.

Although the rising hemlines of the mid-1920s created increased focus on the lower legs and feet, it was not until the 1930s that the high heel and dramatic arch reached notable extremes. Simultaneously, a high platform shoe with a slight arch was also introduced. By the end of World War II, a conflation of a high heel with a slight platform sole had developed. The resulting appearance was of a much higher heel. This combination of platform sole with high heel recurred in the early 1970s, the mid-1980s, and the late 1990s. In its most recent manifestations, the high heel has taken on contradictory meanings. Rationalized as a purely elective decorative artifice, pointed toed high-heeled shoes are worn by post-feminists. On the other hand, several politicized designers, including Jeremy Scott as shown at the lower right, have proposed dramatic interpretations that reinvest the form with misogynist implication, ironic and not.

Edgar Degas, *The Rehearsal of the Ballet Onstage*, oil colors with traces of watercolor and pastel over pen-and-ink drawing on cream-colored wove paper, laid down on bristol board and mounted on canvas, probably 1874. The Metropolitan Museum of Art, European Paintings, H. O. Havemeyer Collection, Gift of Horace Havemeyer, 1929 (29.160.26)

Jeremy Scott, "Body modification" show, 1996, Photograph: © Ali Madhavi, Courtesy Galerie Enrico Navarra

Jean-Etienne Liotard's Orientalist depiction, reproduced on the facing page, portrays a Frankish woman, a non-native resident of Turkey, and her attendant wearing *takunya*, or pattens. This footgear was intended to elevate the feet away from the wet floor of the *hamam*, or bath. The *kuma*, or font, seen in the background situates the two figures in the central part of the bathhouse. Because the woman is fully dressed, there has been speculation that this painting is meant to document a prenuptial bridal festivity. In fact, highly decorated pattens, such as the mother-of-pearl inlaid-wood example shown above left, continue to be worn as part of traditional bridal dress in Turkey, Syria, and elsewhere.

In an eighteenth-century miniature in the British Library in London, a bathhouse attendant wears a similar, but less elaborate costume and pattens at least eighteen inches high. She is serving coffee to a roomful of nude bathers. Like the woman in the Liotard painting, the bathhouse attendant has slipped her extraordinarily high pattens over kid slippers. The bathers all wear more modest pattens, in scale with those of the woman in the Liotard, suggesting that clogs of such extreme height may have been a response to function rather than fashion or prestige.

The ornately incised silver sandals illustrated above center are an exceptionally opulent elaboration on the wood, wood and mother-of-pearl, and wood and silver pattens worn to keep the feet dry in the *hamam*. Unlike the wooden pattens in the Liotard or the higher mother-of-pearl inlaid-wood pattens shown above left, the risers of the sandals have been thickened, and the back riser has been transformed into a full heel.

The heel form appears in the pair of silver ceremonial sandals from India shown above right. Unlike the pattens, these sandals are held to the foot by a knob clasped between the big and second toes. The reeded heel is balanced by a similar front riser. Only the off-center positioning of the knob of the flat sole differentiates the right from the left foot. As with the *takunya*, the Indian sandals represent the footprint as a completely symmetrical shape.

Facing page: Jean-Etienne Liotard, *A Frankish Woman and Her Servant,* oil on canvas, ca. 1750. The Nelson-Atkins Museum of Art, Kansas City, Missouri (Purchase: Nelson Trust) 56-3. Photograph: E.G. Schempf

Turkey, *Takunya* pattens, 1932-44. Photograph: American Museum of Natural History, New York (70.0/5690AB)

Turkey, Elevated sandal, 19th century. Photograph: Courtesy of the Bata Shoe Museum

India, Ceremonial sandals, 19th century. Photograph: Courtesy of the Bata Shoe Museum

The thick soled raised shoe was designed for function: it was made to protect the foot from irregularly paved and potentially wet or muddy streets. But the enhancement of the stature of the wearer also played a role. Developed in the early sixteenth century, the high platform shoe called the *chopine* addressed both requirements.

Because of their height, *chopines* introduced an awkwardness and instability to a woman's walk. The Venetian woman who wore them was generally accompanied by an attendant on whom she would balance. Surprisingly, despite the obvious consequent expense of the practice, Venetian sumptuary laws did not address the issue of exaggerated footwear until it reached dangerous and precarious proportions. The *chopines* shown above left are not as high as the pair depicted in Vittore Carpaccio's painting of two women from about 1500, which is reproduced on page 140. This work, in which the shoes were placed like another of the iconographic clues that litter the painting, includes perhaps the most famous representation of *chopines* in art. In the past, the women who wore such footwear were thought to be courtesans, but that assumption has recently been disputed.

In the Metropolitan Museum's transformative print shown on the facing page, a Venetian woman, the target of a cupid, reveals a vertiginous pair of *chopines* when her skirt is lifted. Her use of a feather fan to fend off cupid's arrows suggests the cool worldliness of the professional beauty, but it is impossible to say for sure. The elaborate dress of a respectable Venetian noblewoman was almost indistinguishable from the dress of the successful courtesan. So vexing was the confusion that sumptuary laws were created to address the problem, and at one point, courtesans were precluded from wearing dresses made of silk as well as virtually all jewelry.

It was once thought that the very high *chopines*, twenty inches in the example shown above right, were the accoutrements of the courtesan and were intended to establish her highly visible public profile. However, contemporary sixteenth-century accounts suggest that the height of the *chopines* may have been associated with the level of nobility and grandeur of the Venetian woman who wore them rather than with any imputation as to her profession.

Facing page: Artist unknown, Venetian woman with *chopines*, two views, engraving, ca. 1590. The Metropolitan Museum of Art, Drawings and Prints, Elisha Whittelsey Collection, Elisha Whittelsey Fund, 1955 (55.503.30)

Venetian, *Chopines,* ca. 1600. The Metropolitan Museum of Art, The Costume Institute, Purchase, Irene Lewisohn Bequest Fund, 1972 (1973.114.4ab). Photograph: Karin L. Willis, The Photograph Studio, The Metropolitan Museum of Art

Venetian, Twenty-inch *chopines,* 16th century. Photograph: Museo Correr di Veneziani

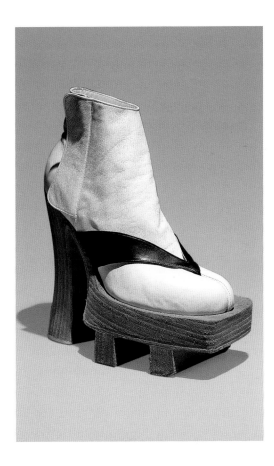
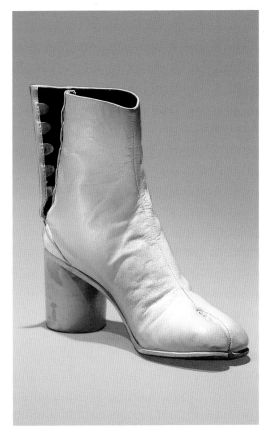

Like Turkish *takunya*, Japanese *geta*, or wooden clogs, are typically elevated on two flat wooden slats. Variations occur with work clogs and more formal examples in which the number and shape of the risers differ or in which the sole and risers are thickened and lacquered. For example, the *geta* of sushi chefs are sometimes a foot high. Such elevation was designed not only to keep their *tabi*-ed, or stockinged, feet clear from spillage but also to equalize their height with the raised serving counter traditional for the sushi bar. While both ordinary and work-associated footwear are generally made of unvarnished wood, clogs worn by geisha are often not only lacquered but also ornamented.

With the exception of the sushi chef's towering footwear, *oiran*, or courtesans, like the one shown on the facing page, wore the highest *geta*. Like the *chopines* of Venetian women, the clogs of the *oiran* required that an attendant accompany her on her ceremonial parade through the streets. In an elaborate display of her beauty and extravagant dress, the *oiran*'s slow progress was characterized by a novel gait. Because of her four-inch-high *dochu-geta*, her heavily padded kimono, and her gigantic *obi*—worn in front rather than in the back as was most traditional— the *oiran* stepped forward with her right foot and then dragged her left foot to meet it. She then stepped forward with her left foot and dragged her right foot into place. This alternation of steps in a figure-8 pattern established the pace and equilibrium of her walk.

As seen in the illustration above left, Byron Lars blended aspects of a 1970s platform shoe and a Japanese workman's clog. His white leather shoe with black leather trompe-l'oeil strap approximates the *tabi*, the traditional Japanese woven bifurcated-toe sock, and the *geta* strap. The wooden sole has the two flat risers typical of the *geta*, but they have migrated to the front part of the shoe. A flared heel raises the back of the foot.

The highly conceptual designer Martin Margiela created the boot with a Dadaist transposition shown above right. He took the structure of a *tabi*, interpreted it in leather, and added a cylindrical heel. Even the ankle closures of rounded brass tabs and looped eyelets conform in principle to the Japanese model. Interestingly, the heel is formed like the plug attached to a Chinese lotus shoe to adapt it for walking.

Facing page: Artist unknown, School unknown, Oiran wearing *Dochu-geta*, 1870s–90s. The Metropolitan Museum of Art, Department of Photographs, Gift of Mrs. Morris Hamilton, 1947 (1991.1073.93). Photograph: Mark Morosse, The Photograph Studio, The Metropolitan Museum of Art

Byron Lars, "Geta" shoe, spring-summer 1994. The Metropolitan Museum of Art, The Costume Institute, Gift of Byron Lars, 1997 (1997.246c,d). Photograph: Karin L. Willis, The Photograph Studio, The Metropolitan Museum of Art

Martin Margiela, "Tabi" boot, 1993. The Museum at the Fashion Institute of Texhnology, New York, Donation from the Archives of Maison Martin Margiela, Paris (97.82.1b,c). Photograph: Karin L. Willis, The Photograph Studio, The Metropolitan Museum of Art

Manchu, Platform shoes, Qing Dynasty
(1644-1911). The Metropolitan Museum of
Art, The Costume Institute. Left: Gift of Mrs.
Van S. N. Merle Smith, 1941
(CI 41.110.272a,b). Center: Gift of Mrs.
A. R. Von Hemert, 1947 (CI47.42.2a,b).
Right: Glenn Roberts Collection. Photograph:
Karin L. Willis, The Photograph Studio, The
Metropolitan Museum of Art

Facing page: Hsun-ling, *Empress Dowager
Cixi and the Imperial Eunuchs,* 1902-08.
Freer Gallery of Art, Smithsonian Institution,
Washington, D.C., collection: Tz-u-hsi (Cixi),
Empress Dowager of China, 1835-1908.
Photograph: Freer Gallery of Art and Arthur
M. Sackler Gallery Archives, Smithsonian
Institution, Washington, D.C.

While the platform shoe may be born of function, considerations of social status and the association of height with fashionable beauty encourage its elevation beyond practical necessity. The Manchu in China, for all their embrace of important Chinese institutions and cultural forms, never subscribed to certain fashions. Most notable was their almost universal rejection of the practice of foot-binding.

Manchu footwear, for men and women, however, had its own peculiarities. The foot itself was not reshaped, but the soles were platforms raised from two to four inches high. Men's shoes had a black sateen slipper-shaped upper, with a painted white platform angled inward at the front. As illustrated above, women's shoes were more elaborate, with exquisitely embroidered motifs on colored silk uppers. Unlike the men's platforms, a central waisted pedestal of varying height supported the women's shoes.

The hoof-like spread of the platform seems appropriate for the Manchu, a nomadic people who were accomplished horsemen, but the form of the pedestal, like the splayed risers of the Turkish *takunya* or the platforms of Venetian *chopines*, are for stability and are not an ethnographic allusion.

In the photograph of the seated Empress Dowager Cixi reproduced on the facing page, her feet peek out below her hem. When she was standing, only the whitened soles of her platform shoes were visible, giving the impression of a diminished support for her bulky, multirobed form. In their own way, the Manchu platforms conformed to and conveyed the Chinese preference for the tiny foot and a tentative gait.

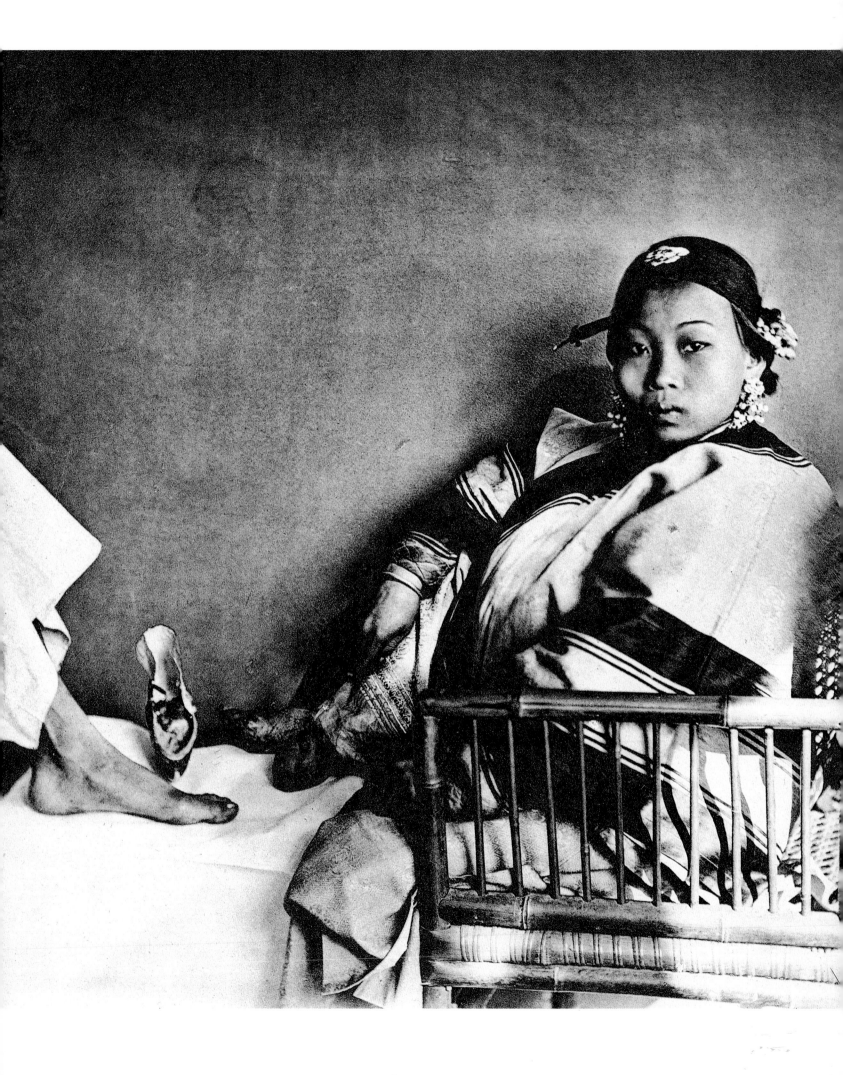

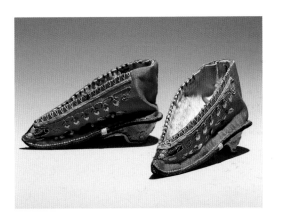  

The practice of foot-binding is shrouded in myth and apocrypha. What is known is that by the thirteenth century, it had come to be a widely practiced custom among Chinese women. Young girls from the ages of four to seven, while their bones were still malleable, began the two-year binding process that bent, twisted, and compressed the feet.

To achieve the ideal length of three inches or less at maturity, the toes, with the exception of the big toe, were bent under the front pad of the foot. This is seen in the photograph of an unbound lotus foot on the facing page. At the same time, the forepart of the foot was pulled back to touch the heel, folding it in half. In the process, which required a continual changing of the binding cloths and cleaning of the foot, a certain amount of putrefaction occurred.

Because the foot was reshaped even as it was growing, there is surprisingly little difference in length between the shoes of a child and those of a mature woman. The size of the Golden Lotus, as the bound foot was euphemistically called, was predicated on the final collapsed footprint that was comprised of the big toe, a small portion of the front sole and underturned toes that were not pressed up against the heel, and the heel itself.

The shoes were often made of expensive highly colored silk brocades and velvets, with heavily embroidered designs incorporating flowers and Taoist symbols of prosperity and happiness. The style of the shoes varied from region to region, particularly in the shaping of the sole. Although it is impossible to say with any certainty, the beautifully embroidered pair of shoes shown above left is likely to be from an earlier stage in the binding process, given the relatively shallow depth of its uppers. A more mature foot bent into the Golden Lotus's final mounded form, as represented by the cerise velvet bridal shoes seen above center, required deeper sides to cover the binding wraps. The whole cycle of a Chinese woman's life—as exemplified above right, even mourning and death—was represented in her shoes. They were an iconography attached to her feet.

Facing page: John Thomson, Unbound lotus foot, 1870s-90s. The Metropolitan Museum of Art, Photographs, Elisha Whittelsey Collection, Elisha Whittelsey Fund, 1971 (1971.635.2). Photograph: Mark Morosse, The Photograph Studio, The Metropolitan Museum of Art

Chinese, Child's lotus shoes, 1870s-1910s. Glenn Roberts Collection. Photograph: Karin L. Willis, The Photograph Studio, The Metropolitan Museum of Art

Chinese, Bride's lotus shoes, 1900-31. American Museum of Natural History, New York (70/1522AB). Photograph: Karin L. Willis, The Photograph Studio, The Metropolitan Museum of Art

Chinese, Mourning lotus shoes, 1870s-1910s. Glenn Roberts Collection. Photograph: Karin L. Willis, The Photograph Studio, The Metropolitan Museum of Art

One of the most peculiar and unquestioned aspects of footwear is its abstraction of the foot into a symmetrical form. Shoe styles have historically shifted back and forth from squared, rounded, or pointed toes. Of the three styles, it is the pointed toe centered on the foot that is the least reflective of the actual anatomy of the bare foot. The pointed toe was a mutable detail. As shown above left in an example from India, it was elongated to the extent that its tip curled back on itself.

In its extreme manifestation, the attenuated toe was incorporated into the leg hose, stuffed at the tip, and anchored to the lower leg or waist of the wearer. Called the *poulaine* or *crackowe*, this form of pointed toed shoe reached its most exaggerated dimensions in the late fourteenth and the fifteenth centuries. As the manuscript leaf reproduced on the facing page shows, the style was affected by dandyish courtiers. It was perhaps inevitably the subject of censure by the Catholic Church and was included in the proscriptions of sumptuary laws.

Footwear with long, pointed, and upturned toes goes back to the ancient Egyptians, who had palm leaf sandals with soles that tapered to a point and were bent back and anchored to the footstraps. Slippers with undersoles revealed at the upturn of their "Turkish" toes are still the traditional footwear in much of the Muslim world. The straw shoe shown above center, probably from Serbo-Croatia, reflects either the persistence of the medieval *poulaine* or more likely, the influence of the Ottoman Turks. Roger Vivier, the shoe designer for Christian Dior from the 1940s to the 1960s, was known for his exquisite forms and extravagant materials. In his evening pump illustrated above right, he took the upturned toe and the turquoise-blue associated with glazes and semiprecious stones from the Middle East to create his *dix-huitième* version of an Orientalist slipper. The sleek contours of Vivier's shoes invariably narrowed the natural spread of the unshod foot.

Facing page: Artist unknown, *John of Gaunt Dining with the King of Portugal*, detail, manuscript, 15th century. Photograph: The British Library / Heritage Images

Northern India, *Ghatela*, 19th century. Bata Shoe Museum. Photograph: Courtesy of the Bata Shoe Museum

Probably Serbo-Croatia, Shoe, 20th century. The Metropolitan Museum of Art, The Costume Institute, Museum Accession

Roger Vivier for Christian Dior, Evening pump, 1961. The Metropolitan Museum of Art, The Costume Institute, Gift of Valerian Stux, 1980 (1980.597.4a). Photograph: Karin L. Willis, The Photograph Studio, The Metropolitan Museum of Art

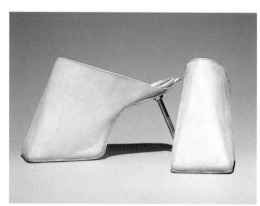

Top left: Weston, Ankle boots, ca. 1920. The Museum at the Fashion Institute of Technology, New York, Museum Purchase (P89.40.37). Photograph: Karin L. Willis, The Photograph Studio, The Metropolitan Museum of Art

Top right: Pierre Cardin and Carlos Peñafiel, Man's shoes, 1986. The Museum at the Fashion Institute of Technology, New York, Gift of Richard Martin (87.16.1). Photograph: Karin L. Willis, The Photograph Studio, The Metropolitan Museum of Art

Lower left: Vivienne Westwood, High-heeled mules, spring-summer 2000. The Museum at the Fashion Institute of Technology, New York, Gift of Vivienne Westwood (2000.30.1). Photograph: Karin L. Willis, The Photograph Studio, The Metropolitan Museum of Art

Lower right: Benoît Méléard for Alexander McQueen, Screw-heeled shoes, spring-summer 2001. Courtesy of Alexander McQueen. Photograph: Karin L. Willis, The Photograph Studio, The Metropolitan Museum of Art

Facing page: René Magritte, *Le Modèle Rouge,* oil on canvas, 1935. Photograph: Giraudon / Art Resource, New York

In René Magritte's painting, reproduced on the facing page, Surrealist *frisson* is precipitated by the vivification of the inanimate. Shoe leather is made to resemble a man's flayed skin. This work plays on the migration and persistence of the body's form in clothing, but it also alludes to the morphological discrepancy between the shoe and the foot. Even broad-toed shoes have been as nonconforming to the foot as the pointed-toed styles. However, because the widening of the foot from heel to toe is in direct opposition to tapering shoes, wide-fronted squared or rounded forms suggest a greater accommodation to the anatomy. But even these more forgiving styles have succumbed to fashion's impulse for elaboration and novel permutations. As recently as the 1920s, as illustrated above at top left, men's shoes, generally more concerned with comfort than artifice, had a dog-nosed profile at the toe.

Contemporary designers seeking a more ergonomically sound form have created shoes in the tradition of Magritte. As seen above at top right, Pierre Cardin, in collaboration with Carlos Peñafiel, modified the footprint of men's shoes only slightly. But he suggested a more natural shape than is actually created by indicating the toes of the foot in clear relief. As shown above at bottom left, Vivienne Westwood took high-heeled mules and anthropomorphized the vamp with a similarly modeled toe-cap. In one regard, the shoe has been made to conform to the contours of the foot, but in another, it does not. The effect of this high-heeled foot is as unnerving as Magritte's transmutated boots.

In his screw-heeled shoes shown above at bottom right, Benoît Méléard for Alexander McQueen carries the irony of a capacious vamp wedded to a destabilizing heel. In this instance, the subtext of physical discomfort and psychological violence, which McQueen sometimes introduces into his critique of the fashion system, is made explicit. For all its ostensible facilitation of the foot's spread, the long, screw-heel creates an angle that inevitably drives the foot into the vamp. With the additional instability of the thin heel centered on the arch, the clog-like form of the shoe is a mask for the *en-pointe*-style drumming required of the toes of ballerinas. Still, the tottering steps induced by the hoof-shoes also betray a suggestion of the erotic vulnerability evinced in the walk of Chinese women with bound feet—or in the more explicit provocation of the buttock-churning mince of a stiletto-heeled Marilyn Monroe.

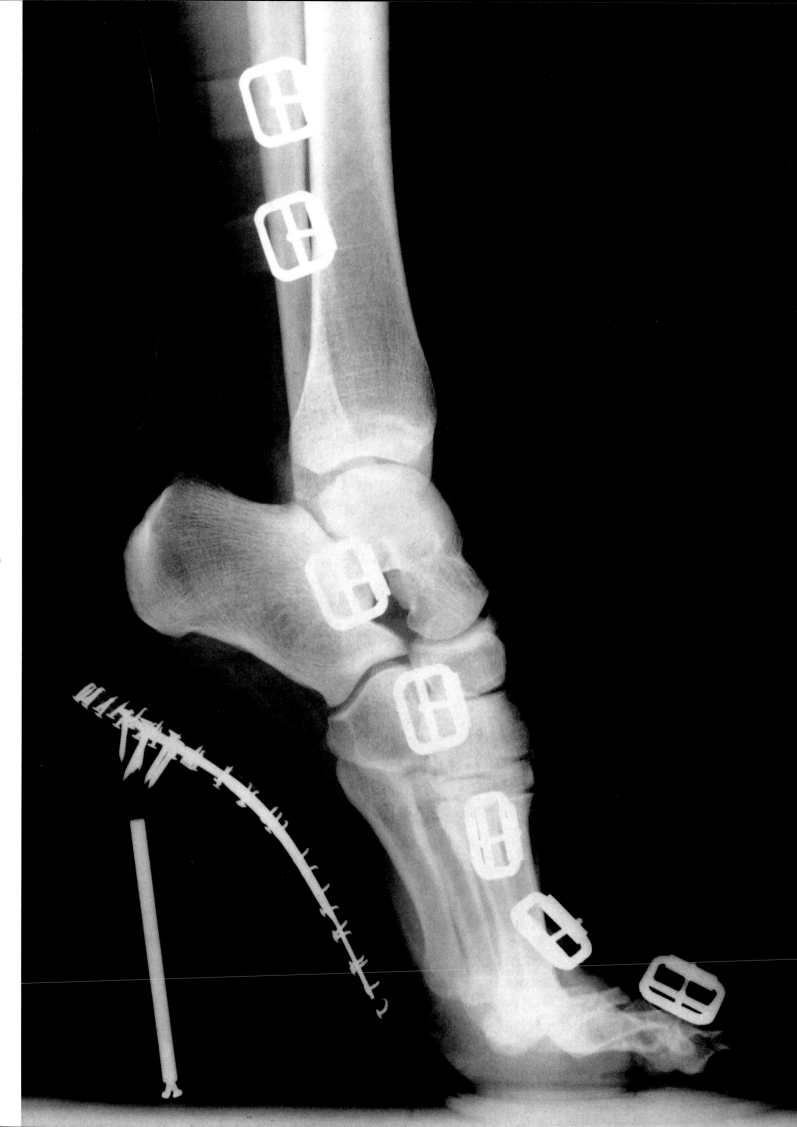

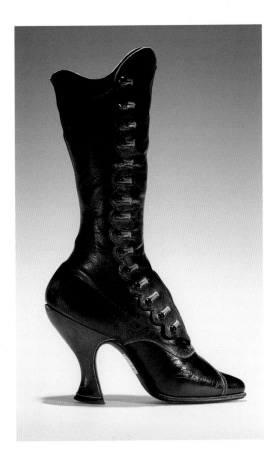

Relatively low heels, one-to-two inches high, were introduced into male and female footwear in the seventeenth century. The wider stacked heel of that date, however, slowly evolved in women's shoes of the eighteenth century into a taller, narrower and waisted heel. It was not until the late nineteenth century that the height of the heel, supported by a steel shank as illustrated above left, accommodated the formation of a more severe arch to the foot. As exemplified in the Ferragamo pumps shown above at top right, both the heel and the arch compressed in the 1930s and 1940s. In the 1940s, the arch was so pronounced that the toes balanced much of the weight.

Popularized in the 1950s, the stiletto, or spike heel, is a nearly invisible support that introduced a hobbling sway to a woman's walk. The X ray reproduced on the facing page shows the weight of the body as it impacts the foot in a stiletto-heeled boot. The line of buckles serves as a directional, indicating the point of greatest pressure at the front pad and toes. The result is not like the unbearable pressure on a bound foot, which terminates in the toes folded under the front pad. Despite this difference, the extraordinary reshaping of the Golden Lotus foot is not so removed in its profile from the almost vertical outline of the foot seen in the X ray of the stiletto-heeled boot.

The most significant aesthetic innovation of the high heel was not its height but its ability to attenuate almost into insubstantiality. The stiletto heel was physically reduced to a nail-like thinness. Given that this style of shoe is a common object of fetishism, the stiletto's dangerous taper has encouraged a reading of sadomasochistic potential.

Facing page: Helmut Newton, X ray of foot in high-heeled shoe. Copyright © Helmut Newton. Courtesy: de Pury & Luxembourg

Jack Jacobus, Boot, 1895-1900. The Museum at the Fashion Institute of Technology, New York, Gift of the Victoria & Albert Museum (71.202.16). Photograph: Karin L. Willis, The Photograph Studio, The Metropolitan Museum of Art.

Top right: Salvatore Ferragamo, Pump, ca. 1938. The Museum at the Fashion Institute of Technology, New York, Gift of Sally Cary Iselin (71.213.44). Photograph: Karin L. Willis, The Photograph Studio, The Metropolitan Museum of Art

Lower right: Herbert Levine, Stiletto-heeled pump, 1950s. The Metropolitan Museum of Art, The Costume Institute, Gift of Herbert Levine, Inc., 1973 (1973.276.3). Photograph: Karin L. Willis, The Photograph Studio, The Metropolitan Museum of Art

162

Even as they add to the wearer's height, high-heeled shoes transform the arch of the foot and musculature of the legs. With the rising hemlines of the early 1920s, the female leg was subjected to unprecedented scrutiny. The small foot or "well-turned" ankle had brief and intermittent moments of fashionable exposure in the late eighteenth century, the early nineteenth century until the 1830s, and thereafter, sporadically in conjunction with active sports and walking costumes. But never before had fashion bared woman's knees.

The move toward tiptoe stance increased the contraction and articulation of the calf muscle. It also pulled the achilles tendon into clarity. This barely visible tautening and tensing of the leg can have a deleterious effect over time. The practice has been known to shorten the leg muscles, and in creating a destabilized stance, it can precipitate problems at the small of the back. The more common possibility is injury to the ankle related to the precarious balance of the wearer. Despite the acknowledged discomfort and physical risks, the high-heeled shoe continues to be popular for the extreme arch, the defined contours of the muscular leg, and the additional stature that it creates.

To that end, consider Herbert Levine's topless shoe, shown above right. Such a modestly heeled shoe without an upper introduced the arching effects of the heel with the impression of a bared foot. The shoe has two pads to which an adhesive was applied to bond it to the foot.

The clear Lucite "Pleaser" shoe shown above left is widely worn by strippers and dancers. It has a platform that lengthens the leg, a high arch, and an ankle strap that anchors it securely. All the effects of the heel are enhanced by the visually permeable insubstantiality of the shoe. Cinderella's glass slipper—transparent, exquisitely fragile, and intact—had a subtext of virginal innocence. In the "Pleaser" shoe, the glass slipper has become plastic and far more durable. The flat slipper has mutated into an eroticized high-heeled platform, less about transparency and disclosure than about invisibility and sexual subterfuge. In her interpretation of the style, shown on the facing page, Sonia Rykiel thickened the heel while maintaining the suggestion of sexual allure. The ubiquity of the "Pleaser" shoe in the world of sex workers has invested it with lurid associations. In the work of photographer Jeff Burton, the explicitly erotic and potentially pornographic are invariably oblique allusions. As seen on the previous spread, the wet imprint of bodies, a drink, and most suggestively, a pair of Lucite heels generate a libidinous narrative of L.A. hedonism.

Overleaf: Jeff Burton, Untitled (glass shoes), 2001. Photograph: Courtesy of Jeff Burton

Facing page: Sonia Rykiel, sandals, spring-summer 2001. Photograph: Courtesy of Sonia Rykiel

Anonymous, "Pleaser" platform sandals, 2001. Photograph: Karin L. Willis, The Photograph Studio, The Metropolitan Museum of Art

Herbert Levine, Topless shoe, ca. 1958. The Museum at the Fashion Institute of Technology, New York, Gift of Beth Levine (76.56.17). Photograph: Karin L. Willis, The Photograph Studio, The Metropolitan Museum of Art

More like the *chopine* and Manchu hoof-soled shoes than high heels, the platform shoe is primarily about elevation. Salvatore Ferragamo is credited with introducing the style in the late 1930s. As seen in his ankle-strap sandal shown on the facing page, the platform, if only metaphorically, brings an anchoring weight to the wearer that is in direct opposition to the stiletto heel. With its reconfiguration of the arch and structure of attenuated insubstantiality, the high heel suggests the lifted antigravitational effect of the dancer *en pointe*. On the other hand, the platform announces an earthbound weightiness more like the flat steps of modern dance. Particularly in the 1940s, platforms were designed with a high arch, but as exemplified in the Ferragamo, they originated with the heel elevated only slightly above the toes.

The platform shoe had a revival in the early 1970s. The height of the originals was exaggerated, although the most popularly embraced models conformed to a smaller rather than a larger range of available dimensions. In a keenly intellectual rummaging through historical forms, Vivienne Westwood revisited the platform. The photograph reproduced above left shows the model Naomi Campbell wearing platforms by Westwood. Known for her assurance and agility on the runway, Campbell precipitated international media attention when she tripped while wearing eight-inch platforms in a Westwood presentation. These shoes were viewed as an extreme that had downed even the fashion world's most professional practitioner.

Recently, young Japanese girls called the *koguru* wore platform shoes of towering dimensions as a badge of contemporaneity. The thickness of their soles easily rivaled the Westwood platforms. A municipal ban making it illegal to drive with *koguru* boots was necessitated by the number of traffic accidents that occurred when the footgear was caught between the accelerator and the brake. In the United States, the fad for platform soles has extended to the realm of sports shoes. As exemplified in the photograph above right, this has resulted in an oxymoronic mutation, the platform sneaker.

Facing page: Salvatore Ferragamo, Ankle-strap sandal, 1938. The Metropolitan Museum of Art, The Costume Institute, Gift of Salvatore Ferragamo, 1973 (1973.282.2). Photograph: Karin L. Willis, The Photograph Studio, The Metropolitan Museum of Art

Naomi Campbell wearing Vivienne Westwood platform shoes, "Anglomania" collection, fall-winter 1993. Photograph: Rex USA

Buffalo Boots Ltd., Platform athletic shoes, ca. 1995. Photograph: Buffalo Boots Ltd., London

ACKNOWLEDGMENTS

This volume and the exhibition it accompanies could not have been accomplished without the invaluable participation of innumerable colleagues and friends. Most fundamental are the outstanding contributions of the staff of The Costume Institute. Our conservator Chris Paulocik has made fragile artifacts of the past available to us through her sensitive ministrations. Lisa Faibish has dressed our mannequins with historical understanding and contemporary flair. And as has been the case for almost a decade, Karin Willis has documented our efforts with transformative lighting and deft composition that are her signature. Anna Abney, Amy Beil, Shannon Bell, Stéphane Houy-Towner, Emily Martin, and Karine Prot individually, and more often in seamless ensemble, have gathered the facts and objects that are at the core of the project. Michael Downer, Jessica Glasscock, Dorothy Hanenberg, Charles Hansen, Alexandra Kowalski, Tara McNeil, Miki Nammoku, Maya Nauton, Tatyana Pakhladzhyan, Natalia Rand, Rose Simon, Judith Sommer, Carmela Tigani, Melinda Webber, and Adrienne Yee have facilitated the effort in varied and essential ways with unflagging commitment.

This publication has been nurtured by the Metropolitan Museum's Editor in Chief, John P. O'Neill, whose insights and advice have enhanced the project immeasurably. Gwen Roginsky has coordinated our efforts adeptly throughout the process. Elisa Frohlich has shepherded the book through its production with consistent lucidity and much appreciated calm. The book owes its graphic elegance and formal clarity to its designer, Takaaki Matsumoto, who was ably assisted by his staff, particularly Thanh X. Tran, Delphine Barringer, and Annie Simpson. But it is to our Editor, Barbara Cavaliere, that we are most indebted. She has for the past decade worked on almost all of The Costume Institute's various publications. Her knowledge and rigor have refined the rough matters of *Extreme Beauty* into its final form.

The Metropolitan Museum of Art is a wealth of concentrated scholarship, knowledge, and experience. The Costume Institute has availed itself of expert and collegial support from many of the Museum's curatorial departments—Arms and Armor: Stuart Pyhrr, Donald J. LaRocca; Department of the Arts of Africa, Oceania, and the Americas: Julie Jones, Christine Giuntini, Eric P. Kjellgren, Alisa LaGamma, Virginia-Lee Webb; Asian Art: James C. Y. Watt, Maxwell K. Hearn, Miyeko Murase, Joyce Denney, Alyson Moss; Drawings and Prints: George R. Goldner, Colta Ives, Connie McPhee, Steve Bentkowski; European Paintings: Everett Fahy, Andrew Caputo, Kathryn Calley Galitz; European Sculpture and Decorative Arts: Tom Campbell,

Melinda Watt; Greek and Roman Art: Carlos A. Picón, Sean Hemingway; Islamic Art: Daniel Walker, Annick Des Roches; Photographs: Maria Morris Hambourg, Malcolm Daniel, Mia Fineman. Other departments at the Metropolitan have also facilitated our efforts with ingenuity, humor, and aplomb, despite pressing deadlines and The Costume Institute's often idiosyncratic requirements—Design: Jeff Daly, Sue Koch, Dan Kershaw, Zack Zanolli; Communications: Harold Holzer, Bernice Kwok-Gabel; Objects Conservation: Hermes Knauer, Shinichi Doi, Nancy Reynolds, Sandy Walcott; Operations: Linda Sylling; Photograph Studio: Barbara Bridgers, Anna-Marie Kellen, Chad Beer, Mark Morosse, Peter Zeray; Photograph and Slide Library: Deanna Cross; Registrar's Office: Herbert M. Moskowitz, Aileen Chuk, Nina Maruca, Anne Goslin, Willa Cox; Textile Conservation: Nobuko Kajitani. *Extreme Beauty* would never have happened without the endorsement of Philippe de Montebello, Director of the Metropolitan, and it would certainly be less but for his gimlet insights. His enthusiasm has inspired The Costume Institute to embark on this enterprise of sometimes daunting complexity.

The rich costume resources of the New York metropolitan area have been made available to us by a number of people at our remarkable sister institutions—The American Museum of Natural History, Division of Anthropology: Enid Schildkrout, Ann Fitzgerald, Laurel Kendall, Naomi Goodman, Renée Gravois, Kristen Mable, Ann Wright-Parsons; The Brooklyn Museum of Art: Patricia Mears, Bill Siegmann, Ruth Janson; Museum of the City of New York: Phyllis Magidson; The Museum at the Fashion Institute of Technology: Valerie Steele, Ellen Shanley, Fred Dennis, Anahid Akasheh, Glenn Petersen, Carmen Saavedra, Deborah Norden, Midge Ritchie, Irving Solero.

In addition, the curatorial assistance, the opening of collections, and the sharing of materials provided by the following institutions and members of their staffs have added a great deal to the project—Bata Shoe Museum, Toronto, Canada: Elizabeth Semmelhack, Ada Hopkins, Sara Beam; Block Island Historical Society: Dr. Gerald F. Abbott, Lisa Nolan; Groninger Museum, The Netherlands: Mark Wilson, Kees van Sinderen; Japan Footwear Museum: Kyoko Ichida; The Kyoto Costume Institute, Japan: Jun Kanai, Akiko Takahashi Fukai, Yumiko Yata; Los Angeles County Museum of Art: Sharon Takeda, Mary Levkoff; Mingei International Museum, San Diego: Adrianne Bratis, Martha Longenecker; Museo Correr: Professore Giandomenico Romanelli, Anna Bravetti; Museo de la Moda y Textil, Santiago, Chile: Jorge Yarur-Bascuñan, Mercedes S. Miranda, Nathalie Hatala; Mütter Museum, The College of Physicians of Philadelphia: Gretchen Worden; National Museums and Galleries on Merseyside: Loraine Knowles, Julian Treuherz, Pauline Rushton, Audrey W. Hall; The Nelson-Atkins Museum of Art, Kansas City: Valerie Zell, Stacey Sherman; The Solomon R. Guggenheim Museum: Susan Cross, Karole Vail; Victoria and Albert Museum: Linda Parry, Sonnet Stanfill.

Many photographers and archives have availed us of their images and accommodated our deadlines with remarkable good humor and notable generosity—Advertising Archives: Suzanne Viner; Angeli/Reflex News: Carlo Montali; Art and Commerce: Michael Van Horne; Art Resource: Eileen Doyle; *ArtForum*: Elizabeth Horowitz; Josef Astor; Jørgen Bitsch; Bridgeman Art Library: Marcus Morrell; Jeff Burton; Camera Eye Ltd., London: David Bailey, Iain Mills; Chris Moore Studio: Sam Cawley, Maxine Millar Chrysalis Books: Terry Forshaw; The Condé Nast Permissions Department: Charles D. Scheips Jr., Leigh Montville, Michael Stier; Corbis Images: Tim Barehm; de Pury & Luxembourg: Helmut Newton, Johanna Schultheiss; Fairchild Publications: Jennifer Bikel; The Fashion Group Archives: Lenore Benson; Firstview.com: Don Ashby, Severiana Casinao; Galerie Enrico Navarra: Jacques Ranc; Galleria Carla Sozzani: Lisa Sacerdote; GAP JAPAN: Nobue Isono; Gossard: Ruth Barnes, Angela Massella; Heritage Images: Charlotte Easey; Hiro Studio, Inc.: Hiro, Pieta Carnevale, James Wade; Dominique Issermann; Daniel Jouanneau; Dr. John M. Keshishian; Knight Galleries International Limited: Natalie Knight, Julian Liknaitzky; Nick Knight: Nick and Charlotte Knight, Philippa Oakley-Hill; Kunsthistoriches Museum, Vienna: Ilse Jung; Metro Pictures Gallery: Jan Endlich; Niall McInerney; National Geographic Image Collection: Lori Franklin; National Portrait Gallery: James Kilvington; National Trust Photographic Library: Edward Gibbons, Robert Morris; NEL USA: Wendelien Daan, Victor Alling; Peabody Essex Museum: Marc Teatum; Bruno Pellerin; Peter Fetterman Photographic Works of Art Gallery, Santa Monica: Frances MacLaughlin Gill; Pitt Rivers Museum, University of Oxford: Lynn Parker; Re/Search Publications, San Francisco: Marian Wallace; Rex USA: Tasha Hanna; Robert Estall Photo Agency, Suffolk, UK: Carol Beckwith, Angela Fisher; Robert Graham Studio: Noriko Fujinami; Scoop: Sylviane Giraldon; Smithsonian Institution, Freer Gallery of Art and Arthur M. Sackler Gallery: Rebecca Barker; Patrice Stable; Staley-Wise Gallery: Taki Wise; Storm Photo, South Africa: Mark Lewis, Caroline McClelland; Studio Luce: Paolo Roversi, Anna Hägglund; Peter Tahl; Time Inc.: Doug Bourie;

Timepix: Thomas Gilbert; Wartski Limited: Katherine Purcell; Yale University, Department
of Anthropology: Mr. and Mrs. Leopold Pospisil.

A number of individuals have been particularly helpful in a myriad of ways. From the
beginning, Katell le Bourhis and Hamish Bowles have taken time to offer direct assistance to
our efforts and to contribute their imaginative perspectives on the project. With innumerable
e-mails, Andrew Bolton has ferreted out addresses and connections that have been of incalculable
assistance. Anna Wintour has introduced us to a number of talents and collections that were
previously unknown to us. With one quick associative witticism, Bob Morris instigated the
conceptual process that has led to *Extreme Beauty*. In addition, there are many others whose
contributions were essential to the project—AEFFE: Lisa Lawrence; Axis Gallery Inc.: Dr. Gary
van Wyk, Lisa Brittan; Bühnen Archiv / Theatre Estate Oskar Schlemmer: C. Raman and U. Jaïna
Schlemmer; Chinalai Tribal Antiques Ltd.: Vichai and Lee J. Chinalai; Craft Caravan Inc.: Ignacio
and Caroline Villarreal; Christine Dhondt; Richard K. Diran; Donald Morris Gallery, Inc.:
Steven A. Morris; Gary Franke; Linda Gross; Titi Halle; Deborah Harry; Kristina Haugland;
Beverly Jackson; Martin Kamer; Katy Kane; Dr. Désirée Koslin; Hanako Kurosu; Erika Langley;
Adelle Lutz; Darlene Lutz; Jane Trapnell Marino; Marion Greenberg, Inc.: Marion Greenberg,
Melissa Gellman; Maxfield Blue, LA: Sarah Stewart, Deirdre Wheaton; Caroline Rennolds
Milbank; Donna Pido; Resurrection: Katy Rodriguez; Glenn Roberts; Singkiang: Linda Pastorino-
Coad; Ruben Toledo; Girault-Totem; Mark Walsh; Robb Young.

Of course, there simply would be no *Extreme Beauty* without the extraordinary body of
work created by the following designers, with the assistance of their always responsive and ever
efficient staff—A.F. Vandervorst: Sophie Pay; Buffalo Boots Ltd., London: Hans Kohl; Pierre
Cardin: Jean-Pascal Hesse, Béatrice Bernard-Malty; Comme des Garçons: Rei Kawakubo,
Adrian Joffe, Chigako Takeda, Miki Higasa; Christian Dior: Sydney Toledano, Bernard Danillon
de Cazella, Soizic Pfaff; Jean Paul Gaultier: Héléne Sipicki, Anneliese Heinzelnann, Leopoldine
Leparc; Givenchy: Marianne Tessler, Katherine Weisman, Mylène Lajoix, Magda Solà; Yoshiki
Hishinuma: Daniele Pinelli; Norma Kamali: Hattie Proteau, Dina Welz; Koshino Junko Design
Office Co., Ltd.: Junko Koshino, Katsuhiko Sasahara, Hiroko Watanabe, Satsuki Yoshida;
Christian Lacroix: Jean-Pierre Debu, Laure du Pavillon, Bérangère Broman; Shaun Leane;
Alexander McQueen: Amie Witton; Maison Martin Margiela: Adeline Cousin; Benoît Méléard;
Issey Miyake: Nancy Knox; Thierry Mugler: Marion Daumas-Duport; Carrie Rossman;
Sonia Rykiel: Jerome Pulis; Yves Saint Laurent: Pierre Bergé, Hector Pascual, Dominique
Deroche, Romain Verdure; Jeremy Scott: Pablo Oléa; Viktor and Rolf: Bram Claasen; Junya
Watanabe; Walter van Beirendonck; Vivienne Westwood: Timothy Clifton-Green; Yohji
Yamamoto: Carla Wachtveitl.

I extend my sincere gratitude to all these talented and amazingly diverse people,
whose efforts have been so crucial in making *Extreme Beauty* a reality.

Harold Koda
Curator, The Costume Institute,
The Metropolitan Museum of Art